What's Le

MW01225286

What's Left?

Women in culture and the Labour movement

Julia Swindells and Lisa Jardine

Routledge
London and New York

First published 1990
by Routledge
11 New Fetter Lane, London EC4P 4EE

Simultaneously published in the USA and Canada
by Routledge
a division of Routledge, Chapman and Hall, Inc.
29 West 35th Street, New York, NY 10001

Photoset by Mayhew Typesetting, Bristol, England
Printed in Great Britain
by Richard Clay Ltd, Bungay, Suffolk

British Library Cataloguing in Publication Data
Swindells, Julia
    What's left?: women in culture and the Labour
    Movement.
    1. Society role of women. Feminist theories
    compared with Marxist theories
    I. Title   II. Jardine, Lisa
    305.4'2'01
    ISBN 0–415–01006–3

Library of Congress Cataloging in Publication Data
also available

ISBN HB 0–415–01006–3
     PB 0–415–01007–1

Contents

Preface
May polls and Morris dancers

This book sets out to give an account of what has been left out of Left thought – what has allowed the Left to substitute nostalgia for programme and action, and to continue to address a constituency exclusively made up of labouring men, in spite of insistent demands from other groups (notably women) who recognize *themselves* as belonging with the Left. And, crucially, the book sets out to make explicit what has been left *in* that exclusive account – the shaping versions of the female with which the account is shackled, which constrain, and ultimately disable it.

This is, then, a book with a socialist-feminist agenda, prompted by a particular conjunction of external circumstances. Socialist feminism is the position from which we consistently develop our ideas, and, most importantly, is the frame for our own attempts at political intervention. Within this work itself, however, we have deliberately taken as given – as absorbed rather than directly discussed – the considerable body of recent feminist work with a socialist agenda. We stress here, at the outset, that it is not excluded from the account but is its necessary premise.

It was against a background of feminist involvement with the Labour movement, and sustained by our engagement with socialist feminism and feminist theory, that our own particular project took shape – a direct response to an urgent political claim for our attention. In the middle of our collaborative work on an earlier version of the first chapter of this book,[1] in May 1987, the Conservative Prime Minister called an election, after eight years in power, and at a moment when opinion polls were firmly in the Conservative Party's favour. As we broke off our piece of 'academic' work (or, rather, took upon ourselves additional tasks which for six weeks took priority over our academic commitments) to work for the Labour Party, we promised ourselves that we would take time after the election – whatever the result – to look back at the campaign in which we had been energetically involved, and to consider its implications for what we had been writing at that moment.

The first thing to say, since by the time this is read the 1987 election will have been consigned to the mists of history, is that Labour mounted an apparently spectacularly successful election campaign, and lost. Indeed, the final result gave the Tories a majority which was exactly that which the opinion polls predicted when Thatcher called the election. Yet it remains the case that the Labour campaign was (and indeed is) judged successful by the 'opinion makers' both inside and outside the Labour movement.

We think that we have given an account here (in this book) of *why* the Labour movement clings to the illusion that there is a politics of culture – that politics can be produced to the electorate at large in cultural terms recognizably borrowed from nineteenth-century canonical fiction. The 'success' of the Labour campaign was in the production of a set of coherent images which treated television as the art form which advertising agencies know it to be. Those images were drawn (comparatively effortlessly, by trained 'communicators') directly from that cultural version of class-consciousness which Raymond Williams so convincingly produces as a socialist alternative to 'high' (dominant) culture in *Culture and Society*. So that Labour did not in fact 'market' itself (and ultimately the failure of the campaign to produce the votes was not a case of failing to sell the product to the consumer). We have tried to show that there are historical reasons why the image makers on the Left (inevitably themselves recipients of higher education, largely in the humanities) are all-too-committed to the *realism* of their black-and-white images of satanic mills, and their bunches of red roses – a *moral* realism, which claims a self-evident equivalence between particular narratives of deprivation and poverty and the moral worth of British socialism (the caring party).

This *commitment* to a particular set of evocative images on the part of Neil Kinnock and his team of advisers is in marked contrast, we are arguing, to the strategies used (in both the 1987 and 1983 elections) by the Conservative Party. The Conservative Party did indeed capitalize on techniques learned in advertising agencies, particularly, in the 1987 campaign, in its use of 'choice' – well-tested in consumer marketing – as the pivot on which its media campaign turned. 'Choice' amongst products allows the consumer to dream of alternatives, even when she or he is without the economic means to purchase them.[2] The Conservative Party *can* use television to its advantage, because it is the party of consumerism, and is prepared endlessly to modify the product packaged, to suit the consumer who pays.[3]

Looking back, it is worth saying here that we ourselves found ourselves entirely persuaded by the campaign imaging, for the duration of the election campaign. That, we would now argue, is not at all surprising. We after all (graduates in the humanities, professional educators) belong to precisely the group for whom Labour's moral realism continues to have force, as it offers signifiers – red roses, Welsh hills – for a signified to which we are already politically committed. What we wilfully forgot – despite being in the midst of our critique of Orwell – was that *recognition* was crucially linked to prior commitment. The glamour of the signifiers could be shared with the 'don't knows' (the popularity of the Kinnock family Party Political Broadcast); but it did not thereby command assent (the cross on the ballot paper), except amongst cultural initiates.

We said that when the election was called we were in the midst of Chapter 1 of the present book. As the reader will shortly discover, we end our opening chapter with a quotation from Bea Campbell's *Wigan Pier Revisited*. To make our present point more clearly, we turn again to Bea Campbell, and to her devastating account of poverty and politics in the 1980s.

> I went home to the woman I'm staying with, a single parent with three children aged between two and nine years. She doesn't get a newspaper and had to ask the social security for new shoes for the two children at school where their last pair of trainers got holes. Today she was up at the crack of dawn, 4.30, to make breakfast for her man friend. He'd come round the night before after playing pool, and they'd stayed up late, so today she is shattered. I arrived home at about tea-time, we talked a bit, the children were charging around until about 7 p.m., when they had their baths, and by 9 p.m. they were in bed. By then I was in front of the television with tea and biscuits watching the news. That felt quite odd. I've noticed how rarely women watch the news. There were two major reports on the news, one showing mass rallies in Spain on the eve of the elections there, . . . and

the other on the miners' ballot. . . . . The woman I'm staying with comes from a mining family, and as I watched the news I heard the ironing board creaking in the kitchen. She was still working, doing the ironing at ten o'clock at night. She missed the news. It had nothing to do with her anyway.[4]

Bea Campbell, watching the news, observes that the woman at the ironing board misses the news, and that 'it had nothing to do with her anyway'. That scenario illustrates the central contradiction between producing culturally recognizable images of poverty and deprivation in the 1980s and *experiencing* deprivation. For the woman at the ironing board to vote Labour she would need to see the problems on the television as hers (she would need, in the first place, to believe that she was entitled to the leisure to watch the television). If the News is already 'nothing to do with her', how could she recognize bouquets of roses as signifying (let alone offering solutions to) her predicament?[5]

Inevitably, now, the story of that election campaign is being re-written, and primarily by others than us. Repeatedly, the male Left has reproduced a plethora of discursive analyses around the subject of 'What went wrong?' The type of campaign may have changed, but as soon as the vote is lost, the old rhetoric reappears. One immediate consequence of this relapse into discursive nostalgia once the political *activity* is over, has been that the ability of women members of the Labour movement to intervene productively in the debate has become once again curiously curtailed. We argue in the present book that women are peculiarly well-placed to register the limitations of the conventional Left account of class-consciousness in culture, precisely because the selective nature of that account fails to do justice to gender. In the post-election period we have been forced to recognize that that very insight threatens to turn us as Left women into twentieth-century Cassandras – speaking true, but never to be believed. We are in a position to see with clarity the constructedness of the account, because its terms exclude us. Because it excludes us – is silent on our behalf – our analysis of the problem risks falling on culturally deaf Left ears. That, in itself, we believe, is sufficient reason for insisting upon a peculiarly feminist contribution to the broad Left debate. We have tried to articulate the problem as *we* see it; we offer our analysis as a partial contribution to an ongoing, collaborative struggle for a Left future.

In the wake of the long revolution

We had always thought of this book as one grappling with events and with lived politics. But in the middle of our work on the final chapter an event occurred which could not have been foreseen, but which inevitably impinged directly upon the whole enterprise. On 26 January 1988, Raymond Williams died at the age of 66. It seemed important to us that we did not alter the emphasis of what we had already written (Raymond Williams had himself read and commented helpfully on the first chapter). But given that Williams had been a reference point or touchstone for our argument throughout, and given that, in the course of developing our argument, we had come to see our own methodology as standing in some significant relationship to that of Williams, Raymond Williams's death undoubtedly made a difference.

Williams registered at an early stage in his work that, for working-class men, there was the sense of inequality in culture, which was experienced as an exclusion. In our own work we found that in the corresponding encounter with culture, for women, the sense of inequality carries over, but there is an illusion of inclusion – when not left out, left in in confusingly compromised terms – which raises distinct political and methodological issues. Williams's response was painstakingly to develop an oppositional stance, which could place working-class consciousness in relation to high culture. We tried this (as, we believe, did several generations of women on the Left). But we came to the conclusion that our own position as women was inescapably *appositional* rather than oppositional, and that there must be a different strategy for women – the revolution longer still. Denied the clarity of marginality, and the lucidity of its versions of exclusion, we kept experiencing ourselves as included – but on the wrong terms – and were forced to conclude that women are obliged to articulate their exclusion from there.[6] For women, politically, the problem is this simultaneous recognition of inclusion and exclusion – left in and left out. How do we challenge the version of ourselves that is left in, without being left out?

We have chosen to indicate the difference made by the loss of the British Left's most influential figure of the post-war period in a Postscript, rather than in any additional introduction or preliminary chapter. It will be clear to the reader that what we were writing was in some sense addressed to Raymond Williams, was intended to be a counterpoint to a debate in which he was crucially and formatively involved, but which had, we believed, subsequently been taken in directions other than those which he and his interlocutors had envisaged in the 1960s (directions which from time to time he perhaps found uncongenial). It matters for our own intervention in the debate that no reply from him is now possible, to incorporate in the continuing struggle for understanding, and it also matters that the retrospective accounts of Williams's intellectual importance – most strikingly represented in the flurry of obituary addresses, lectures and articles in the months following his death – are rapidly altering (and clouding) the picture.

It is these obituary notices which we have chosen as the focus for our Postscript. They invoke many of the themes, and quote many of the sources, which we have used here. The tendency of course was for newspapers and journals to invite a retrospective appraisal of Williams's work and influence from someone who had been publicly associated with some aspect of his varied intellectual involvements, and with an associated 'Left' politics; each offering inevitably tended to accommodate Williams, the many-faceted intellectual presence, to that one particular viewpoint. The result is an interesting series of smooth and appropriately sonorous pieces, which silently resolve problems and erase contradictions whose political importance we have argued here to be paramount. By commenting on these we have tried to refocus the debate on the permanent significance of the Williams oeuvre for Left thought – at least for *our* Left thought – as unresolved, as problematic, and as provocative. A significance, above all, which means Left thought as galvanizing towards struggle, intervention, and action, and as committed in its very essence to bringing about political change.

February 1989

Chapter One

Homage to Orwell
The dream of a common culture and other minefields

In the Britain of the fifties, along every road that you moved, the figure of Orwell seemed to be waiting. If you tried to develop a new kind of popular cultural analysis, there was Orwell; if you engaged in any kind of socialist argument, there was an enormously inflated statue of Orwell warning you to go back. Down to the late sixties political editorials in newspapers would regularly admonish younger socialists to read their Orwell and see where all that led to.

(Raymond Williams, 'Orwell', *Politics and Letters*)[1]

The first question that arose in my mind was: what have I to do with Orwell?

(Bea Campbell, *Wigan Pier Revisited*)[2]

This opening chapter is inspired by Bea Campbell's question, as it is, in the end, by her whole book – her (as the jacket blurb tells us) 'devastating record of what [she] saw and heard in towns and cities ravaged by poverty and unemployment', as she travelled in the footsteps of Orwell's *The Road to Wigan Pier*. We, socialists and feminists, found ourselves driven by our delight at her posing that question, on which the book hangs (what, indeed, have any of us to do with Orwell?), to want to explore it further. At this point, at the outset, she answers: 'Only a point of departure. Though nearly fifty years later I have followed a similar route to Orwell's, his book is all that we share.'[3] But when she asks the question again, at the end of the book, after she has struggled to put the reality (and that's a crucial matter) of urban poverty before the reader, she answers: 'The question isn't simply academic – George Orwell is part of our political vocabulary, he changed the very language we speak, and he

1

is a prize in the contest for our culture between the Right and the Left.'[4] We seek here to build on both these answers to that original question, because we believe that they focus a crucial area of difficulty in any encounter between feminists and the Left, concerning culture, and socialism, in a tradition which we shall argue is shared by Orwell and Raymond Williams, as they cast their long, overlapping shadows over debates on the Left.

One Left reviewer called Campbell's book 'a flawed but in parts brilliant piece of reportage depicting a journey through the depressed towns of the North and the Midlands, written from a feminist and socialist perspective'.[5] And he went on (let's leave the 'flawed' for a moment): 'Her chapter on the "Landscape", a graphic evocation of the physical environment of jerry built high rise council estates, with their sweating walls, uninsulated rooms and concrete flaking off like snow . . . deserves to stand comparison with the most memorable of English journeys from Cobbett onwards, and if only for this reason should be read by anybody concerned about Britain today.'[6] So there is a pretty positive response of the Left to *Wigan Pier Revisited* too . . . apart from that 'flawed'. The flaw is in relation to Williams (whose *Towards 2000* is the subject of the same review):

> Williams [suggests] a new form of socialism which might be built around the ecology movement, the feminist movement and the peace movement. Such a change might occur 'when we have replaced the concept of society as production with the broader concept of a form of human relationships within a physical world: in the full sense a way of life.[7]

Campbell apparently fails in this enterprise: 'What Bea Campbell's book highlights is how much more difficult it will be to achieve a new form of alliance between socialism and feminism – let alone between men and women who aspire to be socialist and feminist – than is evoked by Raymond Williams.'[8]

We shall argue here that the tension between this version of Williams and Campbell's enterprise (complete with its invoking of Orwell) lies at the heart of the Left's persistent failure to take socialist feminism to heart. Which is a polite way of saying that it allows men on the Left to explain to feminists on the Left that their approach (whilst interesting – political, even) is marginal, tangential to mainstream socialism, flawed, partial. We aren't speaking the male Left's language, we don't share the certainties (that confident 'writing well' on the issues), of the English male socialist. Or, to quote Stedman Jones again: 'One of the things now lacking within the feminist movement is male speech. Only when men, sensitive to a feminist case, begin to speak out their own difficulties more candidly, can there be a real chance of constructing the socialist and feminist vision of which Williams speaks.'[9] The desire for male speech, the desire to *author* the case – in other words, to write well about it – is pre-emptive. It seeks to compensate for something seen to be lacking in terms of the 'candid' and the 'visionary', when, as Williams suggests, the absence is fundamental to the socialist movement through that very commitment to masculinity. The argument tends inexorably towards the 'literary', towards a particular version of class-consciousness (the *authorized* account), at the very moment at which it is clearest that key assumptions there are profoundly damaging to any attempt to narrate women in relation to the Labour movement (like Campbell, 'his book is all that we share').

Orwell's *The Road to Wigan Pier* belongs to 'the literary', as a key component in the formation of the narrative of English socialism.[10] As soon as we turn our attention, as feminists, to class politics and the Labour movement, we find ourselves negotiating texts steeped in the traditions of the English novel, in versions of authentic working-class experience formed within the dominant culture by an intelligentsia immersed in a late-nineteenth-century ideology of work and (in particular) of the domestic/the family. 'Authenticity' is problematically consolidated between the narrator and his narrative. If the romanticizing of the English working man is a failing of English socialism, it is so in part at least as a result of socialism's having claimed both a set of fictions (late-nineteenth-century versions of work and experience) and an authoritative voice (the voice of the author) in which to speak about them. The question we begin to ask here is: why has the Labour movement allowed nineteenth-century paternalistic fiction to mediate its class history? And the reason why this question is crucial for us is because, within this account, gender is not, and cannot be, recognized as an issue. As soon as gender becomes an issue, the bond with socialism's language of class is inevitably broken (which is why Gareth Stedman Jones's review of Campbell finds her account so fraught with difficulties).

It is clear that there are many converging accounts to be given of the English Labour movement's involvement with a representation of working-class life as a life of 'worth' in the fictional terms of the classic realist novel.[11] For our present purposes we choose to focus on some of the *consequences* of this in the discourse of the left-wing intelligentsia in England in the 1960s – and specifically the debate around Raymond Williams, concerning the relations between class and culture.

Raymond Williams's *Culture and Society* belongs to the Left 'revival' of the 1950s, alongside Richard Hoggart's *The Uses of Literacy*, E. P. Thompson's *William Morris, Romantic to Revolutionary*,[12] and *The New Reasoner's* metamorphosis into the politicized *New Left Review*.[13] In fact, Perry Anderson identified the 1950s as the period when the word 'culture' came to stand for a central, unifying preoccupation in English socialist thought.[14] Significantly, Anderson also goes on to argue that, in the 1950s, English studies was the only discipline in which a coherent account of English society and its class and culture formations *could* be given; the only area of intellectual debate in which the boundary demarcations of the subject did not fragment the discussion beyond the point of coherent analysis:

> It is no accident that in the fifties, the one serious work of socialist theory in Britain – Raymond Williams's *The Long Revolution*[15] – should have emerged from literary criticism, of all disciplines. This paradox was not a mere quirk: in a culture which everywhere repressed the notion of totality, and the idea of critical reason, literary criticism represented a refuge. The mystified form they took in Leavis's work, which prevented him ever finding answers to his questions, may be obvious today. But it was from within this tradition that Williams was able to develop a systematic socialist thought, which was a critique of all kinds of utilitarianism and fabianism – the political avatars of empiricism in the labour movement. The detour Williams had to make through English literary criticism is the appropriate tribute to it.[16]

It wasn't a detour; the pivoting of Left history and Left criticism around that keyword 'culture' (in a silent agreement) has proved to be an enduring source of confusion. In the 1960s it lay behind the confrontation between Anderson and Nairn on the one hand, and Williams and Thompson on the other, over the place of theory in English Left thought:

In *The Peculiarities of the English* [writes Anderson in 1966] Thompson indignantly rejects Tom Nairn's remark that: 'Actual consciousness is mediated through the complex of superstructures, and apprehends what underlies them only partially and indirectly.' He comments virtuously: 'The mediation . . . (is) not through Nairn's "complex of superstructures", but *through the people themselves.*' This 'humanist' affirmation is followed by a trumpet-call to abandon the notion of a superstructure, and to rely instead on a 'subtle, responsive social psychology'. What this amounts to is beautifully evoked by this account of historical causation working through the people themselves, unmediated by social structure, political formations, ideology – or anything more than a moralistic psychology: 'the working people of Britain could end capitalism tomorrow if they summoned up the courage and made up their minds to do it'.[17]

As we shall see, Thompson *does* tend not to notice the theoretical base on which his invoking of a particular version of history and culture depends. But equally, Anderson fails to register that there is a context within which Thompson's calling up of individual spokesmen for an alternative cultural tradition is certainly *not* 'pure afflatus' ('A young left-wing journalist cannot be discussed without evoking William Morris; the comparison is no more than a slovenly gesture').[18]

Williams himself later acknowledged that readers consciously positioned themselves in relation to his early writing, in ways which he had not anticipated (but which we are suggesting was a particularly important moment in socialist thinking in the 1960s). Interviewed by Perry Anderson, Anthony Barnett, and Francis Mulhern (and that matters; Williams is speaking to them and to a recognizable tradition of politics and letters in *New Left Review*) in 1979, Williams returned to the way in which *Culture and Society* had been 'taken up' in unexpected ways at the time of writing:

My primary motivation in writing the book . . . was oppositional – to counter the appropriation of a long line of thinking about culture to what were by now decisively reactionary positions. . . . It allowed me to refute the increasing contemporary use of the concept of culture against democracy, socialism, the working class or popular education, in terms of the tradition itself. The selective version of culture could be historically controverted by the writings of the thinkers who contributed to the formation and discussion of the idea. Secondly, the possibility had occurred to me – it was very much in the back and not in the front of my mind – that this might also be a way of centring a different kind of discussion both in social-political and in literary analysis. What happened, I think, was that the second part of the project, which I had always seen as subsidiary, belonging much more to the sequel of *The Long Revolution* I was planning, assumed because of the moment of its publication a more important function than I had originally intended. The book was not primarily designed to found a new position. It was an oppositional work.[19]

What Williams is registering here is that he wrote in one sense, and was taken in another. That is to say, he wrote from *within* the 'tradition', an 'oppositional' work, which challenged the coherently reactionary account of 'culture' as articulating the values and ideals of the dominant class (Eliot and Leavis), by offering an *alternative reading* of texts generally treated as bourgeois, to reveal, in their inner conflict (the textual version of struggle), 'democratic' values and attitudes. But at the 'moment of publication', the response to *Culture and Society* came most articulately from Left *historians* (Kiernan and Thompson), for whom (as Perry Anderson has astutely noted) Williams's work seemed to offer (was read as offering) a domain – culture – in which politics and 'thought' were finally brought together, and in which a history of class relations could be charted with new clarity.[20]

Williams makes it clear in the *Politics and Letters* interviews that he himself, in his urge to pin down the relations between culture and class-consciousness, was drawn firmly in the direction of the historians in his later writing (starting with *The Long Revolution*, and associated with his expressed admiration for Thompson's *The Making of the English Working Class*). So he sought increasingly to anchor his 'reading' (a technical term for a methodology of analysis of texts within English studies) in social and political history.[21] But his continued commitment to 'reading' and texts took younger Left critics equally firmly in the direction of more sophisticated techniques of text analysis. Perhaps because *Culture and Society* (for the reasons Williams gives above) never explicitly makes clear the need for a historical underpinning to reading, and given the absence of any historical training within English studies (Williams laments its absence in his formation), the result was a Left criticism which in the crucially formative early years once again isolated the text from history. This is how Williams describes it:

> Distinctly, academically one had been trained to study individual writers – this was, after all, what a lot of *Scrutiny* criticism shared with the orthodox establishment.
>
> But, of course, then you can end up with Virginia Woolf, imagining that all the great writers are simultaneously present in the Reading Room of the British Museum working at their desks, and that you simply have to attend to what they are writing. In fact my work on *Culture and Society* acted as a stimulus, a self-provocation, to get completely away from that mode. The ironic thing is that by the time I was reading Kiernan's review,[22] we had already just completed the actual research for the social history of the English writer. That was the work I had immediately gone on to. Eventually, this was to lead to an explosion of the very idea of the text and of the definition of literary studies through the text, which I was not at yet. But by God when I got to it what should happen but a new and supposedly Leftist movement to revive the isolation of the text? It took another ten years to fight that back, if indeed we yet have.[23]

This problematic involvement in a specifically literary critical tradition was from the outset a crucial source of difficulty for Williams's writing in its relationship to British socialism. In an early essay review of *The Long Revolution*, published in *New Left Review* in 1961, E. P. Thompson voices his (the Leftist historian's) difficulty:

> At times in *Culture and Society* I felt that I was being offered a procession of disembodied voices – Burke, Carlyle, Mill, Arnold – their meanings wrested out of their whole social context . . . the whole transmitted through a disinterested spiritual medium. I sometimes imagine this medium (and it is the churchgoing solemnity of the procession which provokes me to irreverence) as an elderly gentlewoman and near relative of Mr. Eliot,[24] so distinguished as to have become an institution: The Tradition. There she sits, with that white starched affair on her head, knitting definitions without thought of recognition or reward (some of them will be parcelled up and sent to the Victims of Industry) – and in her presence *how one must watch one's LANGUAGE!* The first brash word, the least suspicion of laughter or polemic in her presence, and The Tradition might drop a stitch and have to start knitting all those definitions over again.[25]

Thompson reacts to Williams's 'oppositional' account, with a critique of 'The Tradition', fails to identify the literary critical framework, and puts his finger on the fact that this is not the history of the professional historian. This early response to Williams's work sets the tone for its subsequent broader reception.

Thompson attributes this feature of Williams's writing to his institutional commitment – his (for Thompson necessarily suspect) deriving from an Old English University ('What is evident here is a concealed preference – in the name of "genuine communication" – for the language of the academy').[26] 'Preference' suggests that this is a superficial matter, a matter of personal choice, or even taste.[27] What we are suggesting is that this is to underestimate the difficulty. V. G. Kiernan, reviewing *Culture and Society* two years earlier in the *New Reasoner*, had already identified that disembodied voice of the medium as crucial to Williams's account:

> A procession of individuals does not add up to a class. We are not shown the *literati* in their social setting, as a congeries of clans and corporations with specific functions and specific links and points of contact with other classes. There are only scattered references to the particular kind of 'common man' who stood on one side of them in 19th century England; no reference at all to the particular kind of ruling-class man who stood on the other side; and, as the book proceeds from decade to decade, very little reference to the rapidly altering condition of England. As a result these writers have somewhat the style of disembodied intelligences, spirit-voices addressing us through the lips of a medium.[28]

In both cases 'disembodied' expresses some kind of anxiety about where materially the narrative voice is located *in class terms*. Williams's oppositional Tradition claims to identify a common culture which is not the unique possession of a dominant elite, but offers an authentic class-consciousness. But both Thompson and Kiernan want to know what bearing the *narrators* have on the class-consciousness which is being brought to light, and both are disturbed at the 'gentility' of the consensus which is produced. In Kiernan's case the anxiety is about Burke, Carlyle, Mill, and Arnold; in Thompson's case it is again about the medium, but as the voice of Williams himself – where is *he* speaking from, and on behalf of whom? For Thompson this is a matter of manners and tone. Kiernan is clearer that there is a serious class issue here, and that the consensus of the disembodied voices (of Burke, Carlyle, Mill, Arnold) is a *language of philanthropy* deeply rooted in nineteenth-century ideology:

> It must be observed too that the men of culture, denouncing factories and Philistines, were taking their tone a good deal too easily from the landed interests which were their own old familiar employers. Their corporate existence with all its claret and amenities rested far too much on holdings of land – College estates and livings, Church glebes and tithes; in other words it rested on the depressed existence of farm labourers who could be exploited as intensively as millworkers, but more quietly and decently because they could not combine and resist. Men of culture stood in even closer contact with another depressed class, the immense army of domestic servants, which through most of the century must have been a good deal bigger than the industrial proletariat and not as a rule either better paid or better treated.[29]

If 'in the Britain of the fifties, along every road that you moved, the figure of Orwell seemed to be waiting', that was because Orwell so perfectly produces that very 'authenticity' whose class pedigree Williams, Kiernan and Thompson were debating. And nowhere is the idea of a common culture revealed to be more of a minefield than in the Left's attitude towards the ubiquitous Orwell. Orwell is the subject of the final chapter of *Culture and Society*, the culmination of the alternative Tradition. In his book-length study of Orwell, Williams effectively claims Orwell's style of reportage in *The Road to Wigan Pier* as a 'documentary realism':

> But here the political point *is* the literary point. What is created in the book is an isolated independent observer and the objects of his observation. Intermediate characters and experience which do not form part of this world – this structure of feeling – are simply omitted. What is left in is 'documentary' enough, but the process of selection and organisation is a literary act: the character of the observer is as real and yet created as the real and yet created world he so powerfully describes.[30]

Yet that 'isolated independent observer' has a class profile which troubles the critic as it troubled Kiernan and Thompson.[31] It confirms ways of seeing working life from that class position (the 'squalor', the smell, the loss of human dignity), rather than ways of experiencing it. Thompson makes precisely the same moves with William Cobbett – a figure who crops up time and again on the dust-jacket of *The Road to Wigan Pier*,[32] and who figures in the opening chapter of *Culture and Society* – as the spokesman for working-class consciousness at the beginning of the nineteenth century:

> It was Cobbett who *created* this Radical intellectual culture, not because he offered its most original ideas, but in the sense that he found the tone, the style, and the arguments which could bring the weaver, the schoolmaster, and the shipwright, into a common discourse. Out of the diversity of grievances and interests he brought a Radical consensus. His *Political Registers* were like a circulating medium which provided a common means of exchange between the experiences of men of widely differing attainments.[33]

At the end of *The Making of the English Working Class*, working-class consciousness acquires an enduring voice via the literate, the cultivated spokesman. At the end of *Culture and Society*, class conflict is represented in Williams's oppositional Tradition by the commissioned writing of a disenchanted English gentleman. In both cases, a common discourse is supposed to produce an equality of access to culture and experience of culture, in spite of the awkward class/political placing of the author.

Faced with the difficulty of maintaining George Orwell as any kind of hero of the Left, Raymond Williams's interviewers in *Politics and Letters* interestingly displace their unease:

> Nevertheless in the last resort you seem to let Orwell off rather lightly. . . . In fact what you are saying is that Orwell got very tired and his energy ran out. But your language – 'He had exposed himself to so much hardship and then fought so hard' – strikes a note of pathos which seems designed to exculpate him. Now it is of course true that Orwell had fought creditably in Spain, but it is not the case that there weren't other contemporaries who had fought longer and harder for socialism than Orwell, who did not switch sides so easily.[34]

We might well ask what is going on here. Are we seriously to suppose that the least sound thing about Orwell is his flagging fighting spirit?

We can, of course, sympathize with their discomfort, and with their centring that unease on some notion of 'manliness'. As Bea Campbell stresses, the most jarringly discrepant passages in *Wigan Pier* are those purporting objectively to convey the intolerable working conditions of the face-workers:

> It is impossible to watch the 'fillers' at work without feeling a pang of envy for their toughness. It is a dreadful job that they do, an almost superhuman job by the standards of an ordinary person. . . . The fillers look and work as though they were made of iron. They really do look like iron – hammered iron statues – under the smooth coat of coal dust which clings to them from head to foot. It is only when you see miners down the mine and naked that you realize what splendid men they are. Most of them are small (big men are at a disadvantage in that job) but nearly all of them have the most noble bodies; wide shoulders tapering to slender supple waists, and small pronounced buttocks and sinewy thighs, with not an ounce of waste flesh anywhere. In the hotter mines they wear only a pair of thin drawers, clogs, and knee-pads; in the hottest mines of all, only the clogs and knee-pads. You can hardly tell by the look of them whether they are young or old. They may be any age up to sixty or even sixty-five, but when they are black and naked they all look alike. No one could do their work who had not a young man's body, and a figure fit for a guardsman at that; just a few pounds of extra flesh on the waist-line, and the constant bending would be impossible. You can never forget that spectacle once you have seen it – the line of bowed, kneeling figures, sooty black all over, driving their huge shovels under the coal with stupendous force and speed.[35]

The 'spectacle', whilst ostensibly chronicling the appalling working conditions of the miners, actually elevates the working man's manly body in something close to celebration, and of course recalls D. H. Lawrence's heroic figures of masculinity.[36] But Orwell's attempt to dignify the miner by means of a rhetoric of male glamour only seems to succeed in distancing the entire class to the point at which the bourgeois commentator is absolved of all political responsibility for the miners' labour.[37] This is most clear in the way in which Orwell repeatedly contrasts his *own* physique (that of the public-school 'boy') and manual skills with the ideal type – the deprived and underprivileged working man (supposedly typified in the miner) in terms of undisguised awe:

Even when you watch the process of coal-extraction you probably only watch it for a short time, and it is not until you begin making a few calculations that you realize what a stupendous task the 'fillers' are performing. . . . I have just enough experience of pick and shovel work to be able to grasp what this means. When I am digging trenches in my garden, if I shift two tons of earth during the afternoon, I feel that I have earned my tea. But earth is tractable stuff compared with coal, and I don't have to work kneeling down, a thousand feet underground, in suffocating heat and swallowing coal dust with every breath I take; nor do I have to walk a mile bent double before I begin. The miner's job would be as much beyond my power as it would be to perform on the flying trapeze or to win the Grand National. . . . By no conceivable amount of effort or training could I become a coal-miner; the work would kill me in a few weeks.[38]

Or again:

All of us *really* owe the comparative decency of our lives to poor drudges underground, blackened to the eyes, with their throats full of coal dust, driving their shovels forward with arms and belly muscles of steel.[39]

At one level, this fascination with an aesthetic of working-class manliness in Orwell is almost too obvious now for comment.[40] Campbell calls it 'the cult of masculinity in work and play and politics [which] thrives only in exclusive freemasonries of men':

Men who write about miners lavish poetic pleasure on their bodies, they seek to *explain* miners in the language of their statuesque and satanic physique. 'It is only when you see miners down the mine and naked that you realise what splendid men they are. Most of them are small (big men are at a disadvantage in that job) but nearly all of them have the most noble bodies; wide shoulders tapering to slender supple waists, and small pronounced buttocks, with not an ounce of waste flesh anywhere,' says Orwell in *Wigan Pier*. It is a familiar fascination; D. H. Lawrence had it, and more recently Vic Allen in his history of the Left's rise in the National Union of Mineworkers . . . writes about his attachment to these men. They evoked for him images of hard, unrefined men, distinct and separate from other workers, hewing in the mysterious dungeons; they are dirty, strange and attractive because they are masculine and sensuous.[41]

As Campbell further points out, this cult of masculinity has devastating consequences for women:

> Orwell makes miners the core of his chronicle, they are the essential man and the essential worker, but the equation between work and masculinity depends on an exclusion – women. The suppression of sexuality which is material both to his affinity for and his analysis of coal mining is also a suppression of history. The equation is represented as natural, and that gives it the force of commonsense. It is typical of Orwell – recruiting the readers' commonsense to conquer history.[42]

For the most part, indeed, the women are simply absent from his account (or bracketed with children, scrabbling for shale scraps). But at crucial points the woman appears as part of a validation of an 'authentic' ethic (in particular a family ethic) of working men, which Orwell insists is superior to that of the middle classes:

> In a working-class home . . . you breathe a warm, decent, deeply human atmosphere which it is not easy to find elsewhere. I should say that a manual worker, if he is in steady work and drawing good wages . . . has a better chance of being happy than an 'educated' man. His home life seems to fall more naturally into a sane and comely shape. I have often been struck by the peculiar easy completeness, the perfect symmetry as it were, of a working-class interior at its best. Especially on winter evenings after tea, when the fire glows in the open range and dances mirrored in the steel fender, when Father, in shirt-sleeves, sits in the rocking chair at one side of the fire reading the racing finals, and Mother sits on the other with her sewing, and the children are happy with a pennorth of mint humbugs, and the dog lolls roasting himself on the rag mat – it is a good place to be in, provided that you can be not only in it but sufficiently *of* it to be taken for granted.
>
> This scene is still reduplicated in a majority of English [working-class] homes.[43]

This *topos* of the 'comely' family home comes direct from nineteenth-century novel narrative, every bit as clearly as did the working man with the iron biceps, and every bit as effectively, it wipes women from the landscape of class, poverty, and struggle.[44] It contrasts shockingly with Campbell's own observation:

Women are the poorest of all. Women are responsible for family finances but they have none of the power that goes with possession. Having it in their hands never made money their own. A flinch of recognition flits across women's eyes when it comes to men and money. Sexual inequality describes their experience of the political economy of the heterosexual family, it's an open secret. Yet while we readily blame employers for their extra exploitation of women as cheap labour, and the state for regulating women's economic dependence on men, we protect men from the shame of their participation in women's poverty by keeping the secret. Family budgets are seen to be a *private* settlement of accounts between men and women, men's unequal distribution of working-class incomes within their households is a right they fought for within the working-class movement and it is not yet susceptible to *public* political pressure within the movement. . . .

It's old ladies who show all the signs of a long life on subsistence, though they wouldn't necessarily see themselves as having been poor, because their husbands weren't necessarily poor. I spent a wonderful afternoon with some women pensioners in Barnsley. They wear macs in midwinter: many never had winter coats. For them, getting a winter coat was a big thing, it was to many working-class women what getting a car is to many men. No winter boots – everything has to be all-purpose, for all seasons. One eats meat once a week, and only two ever ate fresh fruit. Their handbags are shopping bags, their holidays are day trips, and occasionally going to a son or daughter.[45]

But it is not just that Orwell's account is shockingly at odds with Campbell's, in ways which we recognize as having something to do with masculinity.[46] Nor that the equation of masculinity and work is secured as 'commonsense', against the grain (Campbell argues) of the evidence. *The Road to Wigan Pier* is also startlingly out of line with the diary entries which Orwell himself made during his 1936 journey north – diary entries which are much closer to Campbell's version of that northern 'reality'. Yet it is Orwell's literary *opus* (*The Road to Wigan Pier*) which the Left cherishes, not the reportage in its pre-literary form.

There is little evidence in the diary of any peculiar fascination with male bodies, and plenty of vivid reporting of the physical danger and discomfort of coalmining.[47] Here, for comparison, is Orwell's description of the fillers at work, including the unique diary reference to male physique:

The place where the fillers were working was fearful beyond description. The only thing one could say was that, as conditions underground go, it was not particularly hot. But as the seam of coal is only a yard high or a bit more, the men can only kneel or crawl to their work, never stand up. The effort of constantly shovelling coal over your left shoulder and flinging it a yard or two beyond, while in a kneeling position, must be very great even to men who are used to it. Added to this there are the clouds of coal dust which are flying down your throat all the time and which make it difficult to see any distance. The men were all naked except for trousers and knee-pads. It was difficult to get through the conveyer belt to the coal face. You had to pick your moment and wriggle through quickly when the belt stopped for a moment. Coming back we crawled on to the belt while it was moving; I had not been warned of the difficulty of doing this and immediately fell down and had to be hauled off before the belt dashed me against the props etc. which were littered about further down. Added to the other discomforts of the men working there, there is the fearful din of the belt which never stops for more than a minute or so. . . .

During this week G has had two narrow escapes from falls of stone, one of which actually grazed him on its way down. These men would not last long if it were not that they are used to the conditions and know when to stand from under. I am struck by the difference between the miners when you see them underground and when you see them in the street etc. Above ground, in their thick ill-fitting clothes, they are ordinary-looking men, usually small and not at all impressive and indeed not distinguishable from other people except by their distinctive walk (clumping tread, shoulders very square) and the blue scars on their nose. Below, when you see them stripped, all, old and young, have splendid bodies, with every muscle defined and wonderfully small waists. I saw some miners going into their baths. As I thought, they are quite black from head to foot. So the ordinary miner, who has no access to a bath, must be black from the waist down six days a week at least.[48]

'You can never forget that spectacle once you have seen it', but it is not the *same* spectacle. In the diary physique takes its place on a fairly equal footing with other observed features of conditions down the mine. In *Wigan Pier* it becomes the aesthetic of romanticized manhood: those 'noble bodies; wide shoulders tapering to slender supple waists, and small pronounced buttocks, with not an ounce of waste flesh anywhere'. And where in *Wigan Pier* the contrast made is between the fillers' physique and Orwell's, the diary makes a point of the contrast between their *skills*: 'When I sit typing the family, expecially Mrs G and the kids, all gather around to watch absorbedly, and appear to admire my prowess almost as much as I admire that of the miners.'[49] In a movement which we (like Bea Campbell) are arguing is related to this transposition of observed working practice into a literary idyll of equatable masculinity and work, the literary text erases the graphic evidence of women which is there in the diary:

15 February
   Went with N.U.W.M. collectors on their rounds with a view to collecting facts about housing conditions, especially in the caravans. Have made notes on these, q.v. What chiefly struck me was the expression on some of the women's faces, especially those in the more crowded caravans. One woman had a face like a death's head. She had a look of absolutely intolerable misery and degradation. I gathered that she felt as I would feel if I were coated all over with dung. All the people however seemed to take these conditions quite for granted. They have been promised houses over and over again but nothing has come of it and they have got into the way of thinking that a livable house is something absolutely unattainable.
   Passing up a horrid squalid side-alley, saw a woman, youngish but very pale and with the usual draggled exhausted look, kneeling by the gutter outside a house and poking a stick up the leaden waste-pipe, which was blocked. I thought how dreadful a destiny it was to be kneeling in the gutter in a back-alley in Wigan, in the bitter cold, prodding a stick up a blocked drain. At that moment she looked up and caught my eye, and her expression was as desolate as I have ever seen; it struck me that she was thinking just the same thing as I was. . . .
   They have found lodgings for me at Darlington Rd, over a tripe shop where they take in lodgers. The husband an ex-miner (age 58), the wife ill with a weak heart, in bed on sofa in kitchen. . . . The family apart from the Fs themselves consists of a fat son who is at work somewhere and lives nearby, his wife Maggie who is in the shop nearly all day, their two kids, and Annie, fiancee of the other son who is in London. Also a daughter in Canada (Mrs F says 'at Canada'). Maggie and Annie do practically the whole work of the house and shop. Annie very thin, overworked (she also works in a dress-sewing place) and obviously unhappy. I

gather that the marriage is by no means certain to take place but that Mrs F treats Annie as a relative all the same and that Annie groans under her tyranny. Number of rooms in the house exclusive of shop premises, 5 or 6 and a bathroom-w.c. Nine people sleeping here. Three in my room besides myself.[50]

In *The Road to Wigan Pier* itself, the hopelessly demoralized women of the early part of this entry have entirely disappeared, and here is Orwell's reworking of the Fs's (now become the Brookers) domestic arrangements:

The Brookers had large numbers of sons and daughters, most of whom had long since fled from home. Some were in Canada 'at Canada', as Mrs Brooker used to put it. There was only one son living near by, a large pig-like young man employed in a garage, who frequently came to the house for his meals. His wife was there all day with the two children, and most of the cooking and laundering was done by her and by Emmie, the fiancee of another son who was in London. Emmie was a fair-haired, sharp-nosed, unhappy-looking girl who worked at one of the mills for some starvation wage, but nevertheless spent all her evenings in bondage at the Brookers' house. I gathered that the marriage was constantly being postponed and would probably never take place, but Mrs Brooker had already appropriated Emmie as a daughter-in-law, and nagged her in that peculiarly watchful, loving way that invalids have. The rest of the housework was done, or not done, by Mr Brooker. Mrs Brooker seldom rose from her sofa in the kitchen (she spent the night there as well as the day) and was too ill to do anything except eat stupendous meals. It was Mr Brooker who attended to the shop, gave the lodgers their food, and 'did out' the bedrooms. He was always moving with incredible slowness from one hated job to another. Often the beds were still unmade at six in the evening, and at any hour of the day you were liable to meet Mr Brooker on the stairs, carrying a full chamber-pot which he gripped with his thumb well over the rim. In the mornings he sat by the fire with a tub of filthy water, peeling potatoes at the speed of a slow-motion picture. I never saw anyone who could peel potatoes with quite such an air of brooding resentment. You could see the hatred of this 'bloody woman's work', as he called it, fermenting inside him, a kind of bitter juice. He was one of those people who can chew their grievances like a cud.[51]

Here, perhaps most tellingly of all for our present argument, 'deprivation' is shifted from the physical circumstances chronicled at length in the diary, to Mr 'Brooker''s loss of manhood, as evidenced by the humiliatingly domestic tasks he is obliged to perform. His wife's heart condition has become trivial, 'I suspect that her only real trouble was over-eating',[52] and Maggie and Annie's drudgery has become ordinary domesticity: not 'obviously unhappy', but 'fair-haired, sharp-nosed, unhappy-looking'. Mrs F's tyranny has become 'nagged her in that . . . loving way that invalids have'.

Campbell's response to *Wigan Pier* is to account for the difference between its manner of addressing poverty and her own in terms of the different class origins and genders of the authors:

> He was an upper-class old Etonian, a southern ex-colonial. I'm from the North, from the working class. Like him, I'm white, I'm a jobbing journalist; unlike him I'm a feminist. I grew up among the kind of communists and socialists who guided him into the working-class communities and who staff some of their struggles. Politics is to me what privilege is to him.[53]

What we are suggesting is that something else mediates Orwell's experiences on his northern journey – a mediation which is part of the production of the text of *Wigan Pier* for the reader as standing in an identifiable relationship to a specifically literary tradition. And at this point we should point out that we have deliberately chosen not to speak of this mediation in terms of 'the dominant culture', in spite of the awkwardness of that notion of the 'literary'. The examples just given do show (rather graphically, we think) Orwell deliberately crafting his published account in terms of cultural forms and practices by means of which a position of privilege is produced as 'commonsense' (they are of course present in the diary, but are consciously honed into 'commanding' form in *Wigan Pier*). But if we label these as 'dominant culture', we tend to imagine we hold ourselves aloof from the seductive power of such discursive strategies, either as historians or as critics (and these are the categories of Left intellectual to which we have been giving attention).[54] Whereas we are trying here to suggest that in its attachment to Orwell as part of a counter-tradition which provides access to 'authenticity' (even when that attachment is produced as some kind of *reluctance*, as in the *Politics and Letters* interview), the Left continues to shape and validate its own authored/authorized version of 'experience' in those terms.[55]

The Left's commitment since the 1960s to *fiction* as the authorized version of class-consciousness for English socialism has continually clouded the issues. It has recirculated the arguments around the literary (as the 'totalizing' context) without Williams's reservations. Some fifteen years after the Left historians had first engaged with Williams, in 1976, Terry Eagleton published a version of the opening chapter of his forthcoming *Criticism and Ideology*,[56] in *New Left Review*, under the title, 'Criticism, and politics: the work of Raymond Williams', which took Williams to task in ways which are entirely symptomatic of the problem.[57] In this 'aggressive survey' (as Anthony Barnett later called it),[58] Eagleton – a practising literary critic – drew explicit attention to the fact that in order to see the significance of Williams's work it was necessary to take into account its position in relation to a particular school of literary criticism (though as we suggested earlier, Perry Anderson had already pointed out the crucial role literary criticism in general, and Williams's criticism in particular, had played as the 'totalizing' context for twentieth-century English socialist thought):[59]

In [*Culture and Society*] Williams sought to extend and connect (symptomatic terms in his writing) what was still in many ways a Leavisian perspective to a 'socialist humanism' radically hostile to *Scrutiny*'s political case. What the work did, in effect, was to take the only viable tradition Williams had to hand – the Romantic radical-conservative lineage of nineteenth-century England – and extract from it those 'radical' elements which could be ingrafted into a 'socialist humanism'. That is to say, the elements extracted – tradition, community, organism, growth, wholeness, continuity and so on – were interlocked with the equally corporatist, evolutionary discourse of labourism, so that the organicism of the one language reproduced and elaborated the organicism of the other. The book thus paradoxically reproduced the nineteenth-century bourgeois exploitation of Romantic radical-conservative ideology for its own ends – only this time the ends in question were socialist. And it could do so, of course, because the working-class movement is as a matter of historical fact deeply infected by the Carlylean and Ruskinian ideologies in question. It was a matter of the book *rediscovering* that tradition, offering it as a richly moral and symbolic heritage to an ideologically impoverished labour movement, just as in nineteenth-century England that tradition became an ideological crutch to the industrial bourgeoisie. The manoeuvre was enabled, of course, by the fact that both Romantic and labourist ideologies are in partial conflict with bourgeois hegemony; but it is precisely that partiality which allows them to embrace. Neither tradition is purely antagonistic to bourgeois state power: the first preserves it by displacing political analysis to a moralist and idealist critique of its worst 'human' effects, the second seeks to accommodate itself within it. What the book did, then, was in one sense to consecrate the reformism of the labour movement, raise it to new heights of moral and cultural legitimacy, by offering to it values and symbols drawn in the main from the tradition of most entrenched political reaction.[60]

This passage is worth quoting here at length because of the way in which Eagleton polarizes Williams's critical practice and his politics. Eagleton represents Williams as appropriating a set of terms from the 'Romantic radical-conservative lineage of nineteenth-century England', to construct a 'socialist humanism' polluted by bourgeois values and ideology. In so doing Eagleton makes Williams's prior literary critical practice formative of his subsequent political outlook (which for historical reasons aligns deceptively well with that 'romantic radical-conservative' one). It is surely ironical that it should be a Left *critic* who fractures Williams's carefully sustained connection between his criticism and his politics – the politics *in* the criticism; the critical practice as uncovering a basis for broader consensus within the hitherto protected enclosure of 'culture'. It was surely significant that Williams characterized his first encounter with 'culture' as one of inequality and exclusion:

Culture was the way in which the process of education, the experience of literature, and – for someone moving out of a working-class family to a higher education – inequality, came through. What other people, in different situations, might experience more directly as economic or political inequality, was naturally experienced, from my own route, as primarily an inequality of culture: an inequality which was also, in an obvious sense, an uncommunity. This is, I think, still the most important way to follow the argument about culture, because everywhere, but very specifically in England, culture is one way in which class, the fact of major divisions between men, shows itself.[61]

For Williams the class politics was built into that initial encounter, the literary was simply a peculiarly rich source of political engagement and understanding:

> Literature has a vital importance because it is at once a formal
> record of experience, and also, in every work, a point of intersec-
> tion with the common language that is, in its major bearings,
> differently perpetuated. The recognition of culture as the body of
> all these activities, and of the ways in which they are perpetuated
> and enter into our common living, was valuable and timely. But
> there was always the danger that this recognition would become
> not only an abstraction but in fact an isolation. To put upon
> literature, or more accurately upon criticism, the responsibility of
> controlling the quality of the whole range of personal and social
> experience, is to expose a vital case to damaging misunderstan-
> ding.[62]

Here, Williams is taking issue with a particular tradition from
Coleridge, through Arnold, to that pervasive dimension of Leavis
which leaves his potential radicalism forgotten in favour of the
celebration of an exclusive minority culture, maintained by its
commitment to the literary.[63] Williams points out that, whilst Eliot
comes clean about this foregrounding of the literary, Leavis operates
it, possibly more dangerously, as an assumption: the centrality of
English and the literary. And yet this is the very assumption which
Eagleton is misreading from Williams, and which subsequently led
Eagleton in search of an 'alternative terrain of scientific knowledge',
within which criticism would 'break with its ideological pre-
history'.[64]

We introduce this first explicitly literary critical intervention,
however, largely for the response it provoked from E. P. Thompson.
Thompson, publishing a 'postscript' for the revised edition of his
influential political biography of Morris, took the opportunity of
adding an 'afterword' in response to Eagleton. It concludes:

> The point of this note is to emphasize the *continuing* difficulty of
> the problems discussed in my essay [whether Morris transformed
> Romanticism into an influential politics, or was an isolated
> eccentric]. Eagleton's position is diametrically opposed to that of
> Morris, and arises from distinct presuppositions. Morris sought in
> every way to implant, encourage and enlarge new 'wants' in the
> present, and imbue the socialist movement with an alternative
> notation of value *before* the 'rupture'; and he judged that socialist
> success or failure in this enterprise would affect not only when the

revolution came but what form it would take. In the event, Morris saw (although unclearly) that 'ruptures' in values are taking place *all the time*, and not only during moments of strike and rebellion. If Eagleton is in any way representative of Marxist thinking today, we can expect the argument between traditions to go on. It may have been thought once, by the Althusserian anti-'humanists', that those of us who acknowledge our continuing relation to the transformed Romantic tradition could simply be read out of the intellectual Left: we belonged somewhere else. But that attempt has failed. We are still here: we do not mean to go. Neither the Left nor Marxism can ever belong to any set of people who put up fences and proprietary signs; it can belong only to all those who choose to stay in that 'terrain' and who mix it with their labour. I say this sharply, but not because I think that the argument should be closed. It is a serious continuing quarrel of principles, and, indeed, 'the case of William Morris' has perhaps already passed on into 'the case of Raymond Williams'.[65]

With a characteristically grand theatrical sweep, Thompson takes back Eagleton's critique of Williams's literary critical undertaking, and reidentifies it as an attack on the political integrity of a socialist tradition from Morris to Williams (and, of course, as the rhetorical flourishes testify, to Thompson himself).[66] 'Culture' regains the multiple density of 'history' as opposed to the specificity of 'text'. Left criticism set off towards the 'scientific' isolation of the text in the name of a 'hard' radical alternative; the 'Old New Left' ('We are still here: we do not mean to go'), remained untroubled by that important suggestion of Eagleton's that the roots of their political discourse might bear closer scrutiny.

Ten years on again, is it surprising that Bea Campbell finds herself bemusedly ferreting through the baggage of the Orwellian tradition, for the means of conveying to her reader that 'real', that 'authenticity' of poverty and deprivation which is the experience of women and of non-white ethnic groups? Asked why 'women and the family do not make any entry at all' in *The Long Revolution*, Williams replied that he wished they had done so: 'And I also wish I understood what prevented me from doing so, because it wasn't that I was not thinking about the question.'[67]

Our aim in this chapter has been to begin to offer an answer to Raymond Williams's question, as to that provocative opening question of Bea Campbell's. And we close with a passage from Campbell which conveys more vividly than any more argument of ours what it is (of that 'real' with which she was struggling) that the Left has lost if it refuses to acknowledge that 'literary' in its history:

> I went home to the woman I'm staying with, a single parent with three children aged between two and nine years. She doesn't get a newspaper and had to ask the social security for new shoes for the two children at school where their last pair of trainers got holes. Today she was up at the crack of dawn, 4.30, to make breakfast for her man friend. He'd come round the night before after playing pool, and they'd stayed up late, so today she is shattered. I arrived home at about tea-time, we talked a bit, the children were charging around until about 7 p.m., when they had their baths, and by 9 p.m. they were in bed. By then I was in front of the television with tea and biscuits watching the news. That felt quite odd. I've noticed how rarely women watch the news. There were two major reports on the news, one showing mass rallies in Spain on the eve of the elections there, . . . and the other on the miners' ballot. . . . The woman I'm staying with comes from a mining family, and as I watched the news I heard the ironing board creaking in the kitchen. She was still working, doing the ironing at ten o'clock at night. She missed the news. It had nothing to do with her anyway.[68]

By confronting that initial question ('What have [any of us] to do with Orwell?'), we may begin to find an answer that deals with the political enormity of that final sentence: 'It had nothing to do with her anyway.'

Chapter Two

'In a voice choking with anger'
Arguments within English Marxism

> Sociologists who have stopped the time machine and, with a good
> deal of conceptual huffing and puffing, have gone down to the
> engine-room to look, tell us that nowhere at all have they been
> able to locate and classify a class.[1]

This chapter will concentrate on a long-running argument within
English Marxism in the 1960s, which, we shall maintain, shaped and
influenced those important notions of 'culture' and 'history' with
which this book is concerned.[2] But we begin with an argument
which did not hit the Left headlines at the time (indeed, which was
probably unfortunately masked by the noisier polemic), yet which
was bound up significantly in the same debate, and came (as we
shall show) to exert an equally strong influence. In the 1960s, Juliet
Mitchell, later to become a cornerstone of the feminist psychoanalytic movement in England and the United States, was a lecturer
in English literature, whose political involvement was centred on the
journal of the English New Left, *New Left Review*:

> I was active in the New Left. . . . I lectured in a well established
> department of English Literature (Leeds). In the Marxist meetings
> on the politics of the Third World, in the University common
> rooms I frequented, where were the women? Absent in the prac-
> tices and in the theories. Why this sort of common experience led
> so many of us to feminism at that particular time, though I can
> think of many explanations, I do not really know. Anyway, in
> 1962 I started a book that I never completed, on the position of
> women in Britain.[3]

In the 1960s there was no place for women in the practices and in

the theories of the English New Left, according to Juliet Mitchell.[4]
As we saw, Raymond Williams also registers, in a key published
series of interviews, that there was somehow no place for women in
the 'political discourse' of the period, in spite of the developing
women's movement:

> *NLR*: Given the general sensitivity of your writing to those areas
> which did not form part of conventional political discourse at the
> time, it is very surprising that problems of women and the family
> do not make any kind of entry at all in your work of this period.

> Raymond Williams: I think that is absolutely fair. It was not,
> however, that I wasn't thinking about them. In a sense, the reflec-
> tions then forming in my mind were very closely related to the
> kind of analysis developed in the last part of *The Long Revolution*.
> . . . The emergence of a militant and explicit movement of
> women's liberation from the late sixties onwards was wholly
> welcome and necessary and overdue.[5]

There is, of course, something of an irony in the fact that Williams
is here prompted into acknowledging this 'omission' from his own
work by an interviewing team drawn from precisely the same group
of the editorial board of *New Left Review* who had marginalized
Juliet Mitchell, and assented to a 'political discourse' in which
women were not represented.[6]

In Mitchell's case, in spite of her inability to finish the book on
the position of women in Britain, she did publish a crucial piece of
writing, in *New Left Review*, which drew attention to the problem:
'finally, I wrote "Women: *The Longest Revolution*" – very much
for my New Left friends and colleagues'.[7]

In her title (particularly as she italicizes it in this late, retrospective account), Mitchell acknowledges Raymond Williams's *The Long
Revolution*, first published in 1961, as a formative influence (as she
tells us, she began that ill-fated book on women in Britain, which
we judge to have developed instead into 'Women: *The Longest
Revolution*' in the following year).[8] This allegiance to one of the
intellectual mentors of *New Left Review* at that moment (to which we
shall return in a later chapter) did not, however, shield her from the
confident (indeed complacent) disparagement of some of the
members of the editorial board. The following issue of *NLR* (41,
January/February 1967) contained a frontal attack on Mitchell by

Quintin Hoare (then managing editor) from which the following is a representative criticism:

> There is clearly nothing wrong with Juliet Mitchell's intentions. But I think that there is something very wrong indeed with her basic assumptions and her method, and it is that which explains both the anti-climax of her conclusion and many of the inconsistencies in the article as a whole. It is because the subject is one of the utmost importance that it is necessary to analyse carefully where she goes wrong.[9]

How thoughtful of him. And the crucial dimension in which Hoare finds Mitchell 'going wrong' is that of history:

> We are warned that the article will not provide an historical narrative of women's position. But what, in fact, happens is that she *excludes* history from her analysis. How can one analyse either the position of women today, or writings on the subject ahistorically? It is this which prevents her from realizing that the whole *historical* development of women has been within the family; that women have worked and lived within *its* space and time. We may all agree that her place should not be there, but it is. Any discussion of the position of women which does *not* start from the family as the mode of her relation with society becomes abstract.[10]

'History' as opposed to the 'abstract' are the key counters in Hoare's attack on Mitchell. History, as we shall see later, remains a key component in all Mitchell's subsequent writing.[11] At this point in our argument we emphasize 'history' because between Raymond Williams's 'history' in *The Long Revolution*, and E. P. Thompson's 'history' (particularly, as we shall see, in *William Morris*), Mitchell thought she had found a space in which to produce women in history, and *NLR* took away the space.[12]

But at that moment, Mitchell saw herself clearly as tackling 'women's history' as a Marxist and, particularly, an Althusserian:

> ['Women: *The Longest Revolution*'] arose out of my involvement with Marxism, and my dissatisfaction with any economist understanding of the position of women. The partially buried framework made use of Louis Althusser's work, particularly his then recently published essay: 'Contradiction and Overdetermination'. It was

Althusser's emphasis on the importance of ideology that I found most useful. His definition of it as 'the way we live ourselves in the world' seemed to me an insistent dimension in any analysis of women. It was one strand that led me forward to my subsequent interest in psychoanalysis.[13]

What Mitchell indicates here is that her writing of 'Women: *The Longest Revolution*' coincided with the publication in France of Althusser's *Pour Marx* and *Lire le Capital*, and that *NLR* published the first English translation of a 'representative example' from this phase in Althusser's writing in *NLR* 41 (the issue containing Hoare's attack on Mitchell): 'Contradiction and overdetermination', translated by Ben Brewster (subsequently to join the editorial board).

What makes this public intellectual pillorying of Mitchell by the other members of the *NLR* editorial board the more startling is that they had themselves been subjected to a similar sort of (highly emotional and partisan) attack, only the preceding year. Perry Anderson and Tom Nairn had become the objects of E. P. Thompson's formidable anger (*he* probably didn't even notice Mitchell), and one of the focuses for his hostility was their commitment to the very Althusserianism which Mitchell sees as providing her with the starting point for 'Women: *The Longest Revolution*'. 'In a voice choking with anger', E. P. Thompson launched a violent attack on the intellectual direction taken by *NLR*, initiating a debate which was to last a good ten years, and was to have far-reaching implications for English Marxism:

Early in 1962, when the affairs of *New Left Review* were in some confusion, the New Left Board invited an able contributor, Perry Anderson, to take over the editorship. We found (as we had hoped) in Comrade Anderson the decision and the intellectual coherence to ensure the review's continuance. More than that, we discovered that we had appointed a veritable Dr. Beeching of the socialist intelligentsia. All the uneconomic branch-lines and socio-cultural sidings of the New Left which were, in any case, carrying less and less traffic, were abruptly closed down. The main lines of the review underwent an equally ruthless modernisation. Old Left steam-engines were swept off the tracks; wayside halts ('Commitment', 'What Next for C.N.D.?', 'Women in Love') were boarded up; and the lines were electrified for the speedy traffic from the marxistentialist Left Bank. In less than a year the founders of the review discovered, to their chagrin, that the Board lived on a branch-line which, after rigorous intellectual costing, had been found uneconomic. Finding ourselves redundant we submitted to dissolution.[14]

Here, in the 1965 volume of *Socialist Register*, the contemporary 'organ' for Left intellectual debate, E. P. Thompson publicly announced a close relationship with Anderson (and Nairn), as fellow-editors of *NLR*, only to proceed to denounce them, individually, and at length. Today, 'The peculiarities of the English' reads (as it was probably intended) as a comradely (if slightly patronizing) attempt to stimulate debate between competing sets of intellectual developments on the Left. But to Anderson its hostility was overwhelming: 'No opponent on the Right has ever aroused this fixity of passion and rancour. It has been reserved, apparently, for fellow-socialists'.[15] We might note that Anderson wrote this only months before *NLR* connived in the publication of an article of exactly comparable 'fixity of passion and rancour' against their fellow (but not brother) board-member Mitchell. We shall have occasion to return more than once to this exchange, since it runs through Left debate from the mid-1960s to the late 1970s, although it is hard to keep track of amongst Anderson's and Thompson's publications, because of their tendency to conceal the quarrel itself behind a succession of supposedly general and crucial issues for the Left.[16] And above all because, in our view, it is not possible to understand Mitchell's later intellectual developments without it. And for the present what interests us is the way in which intensity of feeling in the debate – a personal intensity, a sense of an entire intellectual framework under threat (from both sides) – is mirrored in the Mitchell/Hoare exchange, sandwiched between those louder, strident voices. Anderson, replying aggrievedly to Thompson in 'Socialism and pseudo-empiricism' in 1966 (the year Mitchell exposed herself to similarly disparaging comment from *NLR*), felt that the attack extended to everything which he had felt *NLR* had stood for in the previous two years (since the publication of his 'Origins of the present crisis'):[17]

It is doubtless scandalous to be disrespectful to an established historian, pronouncing with all his authority on 'his own' field. On this occasion, however, it is useless to attempt diplomacy or to simulate deference. Haste and passion have produced a curious mixture of blindness to the views under attack, eloquent but irrelevant digressions, and enraged counter-arguments which are often demagogic and empty, and sometimes of a matchless silliness. Worst of all, the whole performance is laden with self-delighted pirouettes, and constant sacrifices of accuracy and sobriety to epigrammatic 'brightness' of the kind that is appreciated on the High Table.[18]

In the last chapter we had occasion to refer to E. P. Thompson's defence of Raymond Williams against Terry Eagleton's attack on him in *New Left Review*, a defence in which Thompson characterized himself as in important ways permanently at odds with the Left tradition of *New Left Review*.[19] But the quarrel with *New Left Review* was a long-standing one, and Thompson's significant distancing of himself from the positions taken by *NLR* in the mid-1960s had by that time consolidated his original falling-out with the editors into an 'English Marxism' demarcated by its refusal of the decadent use of 'theory', as represented, in particular, by Althusser:

> These issues were opened up, more than ten years ago, in an exchange between myself and Perry Anderson and Tom Nairn. In one sense, the critique which the 'second' *NLR* has offered to the provincialism of the British intellectual Left, and to its complacent anchorage in a particular national heritage, has been altogether healthy and challenging. In many areas it has become possible to opt for coexistence. But in other ways coexistence has been made difficult by the gathering Althusserian invective of some younger British marxists against 'moralism', 'humanism', 'historicism', etc. – an invective which seeks, not to redress the insularity, but to annihilate alternative traditions.[20]

It is not an accident that the attack on Althusser is renewed at the moment when Thompson chooses to defend Raymond Williams. That choice seems to us to have been made at relatively short notice. The defence of Williams against Eagleton is tacked on to the end of the long, careful reformulation of his position on Morris, prepared for the new edition of *William Morris*, and published for the first time, separately, as 'Romanticism, moralism, utopianism: the case of William Morris', in *NLR* 99 (1976). There is absolutely no warning of the outburst against Eagleton until the last two pages of this article, and indeed these two pages do not appear in the 1976 edition of *William Morris*.[21] In other words, the defence is in the literal sense 'occasional', and the quarrel still with the journal, *New Left Review*. Moreover, like himself, Williams was a previous editor of the *New Reasoner*, and member of the original editorial board of *New Left Review* (1960–2), now being attacked for his peculiarly English Marxism from the position of continental theory in the pages of that same journal.

We saw in our previous chapter that E. P. Thompson did not always find Raymond Williams's work as congenial as he does by the time Eagleton is turning against his one-time mentor, but it is as if the intervening period has seen Thompson growing into Williams in such a way that, in the continuing address to *New Left Review*, it is Williams who is invoked as the preferred alternative to Althusser. For Thompson, Williams and culture have substituted for and displaced Althusser and ideology. These are the directions in which they, Thompson and Williams together (but not by design – by history and occasion) begin to merge, to shape English Marxism.

And Thompson does shape English Marxism, to the extent that Perry Anderson, who had been bewildered at how venomous that original voice which had attacked *New Left Review* had been, and at the travesty it represented of the work published there, is, by 1980 (responding to the publication in 1978 of Thompson's *The Poverty of Theory*), persuaded that Thompson *is* English Marxist theory:

> Edward Thompson is our finest socialist writer today – certainly in England, possibly in Europe. Readers of *The Making of the English Working Class*, or indeed *Whigs and Hunters*, will always remember these as major works of literature. The wonderful variety of timbre and rhythm commanded by Thompson's writing at the height of its powers – alternately passionate and playful, caustic and delicate, colloquial and decorous – has no peer on the Left. . . . Throughout, his has been the most declared political history of any of his generation.
>
> At the same time, these works of history have also been deliberate and focused contributions to theory: no other Marxist historian has taken such pains to confront and explore, without insinuation or circumlocution, difficult conceptual questions in the pursuit of their research. The definition of 'class' and 'class-consciousness' in *The Making of the English Working Class*; the critique of 'base and superstructure' through the prism of law in *Whigs and Hunters*; the reinstatement as disciplined imagination of 'utopianism' in the new edition of *William Morris* – all these represent theoretical arguments that are not mere enclaves within the respective historical discourses, but form rather their natural culmination and resolution.[22]

Arguments Within English Marxism is not – it turns out – about movements or classes, but is about the texts of E. P. Thompson – texts which, as this eulogy of Anderson's shows, he finds to be bewilderingly a conflation of the 'literary' and the 'theoretical'.[23] Put more clearly, *Arguments Within English Marxism*, chapter by chapter, takes E. P. Thompson's published works, one by one, and subjects them to meticulous, Aristotelian scrutiny. That is why it is appropriate that Thompson's defence of Williams, over ten years on from 'choking with anger', should be one of the additions which is printed in *New Left Review*, and not in the otherwise similar piece which forms the 'Postscript' to the revised edition of *William Morris*. It is in *New Left Review* that, increasingly leaning towards Williams, Thompson lines up English Marxism with 'history' and 'culture', against 'scientific knowledge' and the decadence of 'theory'.[24]

Again in response to promptings from his *New Left Review* interviewers, in *Politics and Letters*, Raymond Williams acknowledges a reciprocity and complicity in this:

> If I had read *The Making of the English Working Class* when I was writing *Culture and Society*, it would have been a quite different book. But then it was part of the conditions of the time that Edward was writing his Morris and then the early work on the making of the working class while I was writing *Culture and Society*, yet we were not in contact with each other – so these crucial conjunctions were never made.[25]

Williams describes himself as having been 'deficient in the historical knowledge' which would have made the writing of *Culture and Society* into more than 'the recovery of a very specific tradition'. The historical knowledge he could have learned from Thompson, had political conditions facilitated those connections. More of this potential formation, of Thompson and Williams, uniting literature and history via the middle term of politics, shows up in what Raymond Williams has to say about the journal, *Politics and Letters*, which he helped to set up in Cambridge in the 1940s, immediately after the war. The intention of the journal was to 'unite radical left politics with Leavisite literary criticism'. Asked to comment on its collapse in 1948, Williams appears to lean towards the position which Thompson represents as one which could have rescued such a project:

> If the intellectuals in the Communist Party had been moving

towards our kind of project, as one could say many of them did in '56, they would have given it much more solidity on the political/economical/historical side. We were all literary people. I have just read Edward Thompson's paper on Caudwell, in which he describes the inner Party arguments about Caudwell in the late forties. My most immediate response was: 'Why weren't you writing this at the time in *Politics and Letters*?'[26]

'We were all literary people'. This, Raymond Williams suggests, is what both defines and constrains the journal, in its endeavour to map Left politics onto literary criticism. It is also what (as Williams repeatedly stresses in the *Politics and Letters* interviews) linked the *Politics and Letters* enterprise with that of *Scrutiny*:

> The immense attraction of Leavis lay in his cultural radicalism, quite clearly. That may seem a problematic description today, but not at the time. It was the range of Leavis's attacks on academicism, on Bloomsbury, on metropolitan literary culture, on the commercial press, on advertising, that first took me. You must also allow for the sheer tone of critical irritation, which was very congenial to our mood.
>
> Secondly, within literary studies themselves there was the discovery of practical criticism. That was intoxicating, something I cannot describe too strongly. Especially if you were as discontented as I then was. I said intoxication, which is a simultaneous condition of elation, excitement, and loss of measure and intelligence. Yes, it was all those things, but let me put it on record that it was incredibly exciting. I still find it exciting, and at times I have positively to restrain myself from it because actually I can do it reasonably well, I think: I've taught it to other people. Today when I am writing about a novel, it is a procedure that comes very easily to me, but I try to refrain from using it. It always tends to become too dominant a mode, precisely because it evades both structural problems and in the end all questions of belief and ideology. But at the time we thought it was possible to combine this with what we intended to be a clear Socialist cultural position. In a way the idea was ludicrous, since Leavis's cultural position was being spelt out as precisely not that. But I suppose that was why we started our own review, rather than queueing up to become contributors to *Scrutiny*.
>
> Finally, there was Leavis's great stress on education. He would always emphasize that there was an enormous educational job to be done. Of course, he defined it in his own terms. But the emphasis itself seemed completely right to me.[27]

Practical criticism and education, as part of a Leavisite package, will concern us more later. What concerns us here is the attraction for Williams of what he describes as Leavis's 'cultural radicalism', an attraction which led those 'literary people' nevertheless to establish their own journal, rather than joining the *Scrutiny* enterprise. But it is the supposed cultural radicalism of Leavisism which leads Williams to choose literary criticism as the practice onto which to graft a Left politics.[28] It is also the limitations of what Leavis represents (which, as Williams says, were being spelt out at that very moment) which led him, after *Culture and Society*, away from *Scrutiny* and towards E. P. Thompson. And one might complete the picture, perhaps, by pointing out that one of Williams's interviewers in these *New Left Review* interviews, prompting the reminiscences about the *Scrutiny* years, is Francis Mulhern, whose *The Moment of Scrutiny* – the first (and only) *political* account of the formation of the *Scrutiny* outlook – had brought him to the attention of *New Left Review*, and ultimately onto the editorial board (were they, perhaps, already looking for a coherent account of this crucial *literary* component in the formation of Raymond Williams?).[29]

Retrospectively, Raymond Williams represents the move away from *Scrutiny* as bound up with the notion of 'class':

> The *Four Quartets* completely dominated reading and discussion in Cambridge at the time. . . . There was a class struggle occurring around those poems and that criticism. Because if you were to move into the world not just of Leavis's criticism, which contained radical, positive, energetic elements, but into the universe of the *Four Quartets*, then you were finished. You were then in the totally conventional post-war posture of the inevitability of failure, the absurdity of effort, the necessity of resignation.[30]

We find the shift here intriguing. In the space of a single page of (extremely acute) retrospective analysis on Williams's part of his post-war intellectual position we have moved from politics, a socialist critique of culture, and the Left intelligentsia, to Eliot's *Four Quartets* and post-war *ennui* in the world of letters. In our view the ease (and perhaps lack of embarrassment) with which Williams can recall this as a vital part of his development (yet one which is consistently suppressed in his writing from the *Politics and Letters* days onwards) reveals the extent to which Literary studies formed Raymond Williams, even as he fixed his attention increasingly on 'class' and 'culture'.[31]

As Williams saw, what is needed to prevent critical reading (which Williams openly admits to be his preferred analytic mode) of Eliot from occluding class (indeed, to prevent it from compromising the critic within the very elite class framework to which Eliot subscribes) is historical materialism, Thompson-style.[32]

We are well aware that in shifting attention backwards and forwards between Thompson and Williams we shift disciplines as well as narratives, and we can feel the strain. The developments we are tracing can, in fact, be seen as a developing inclination to paper over the cracks between those disciplines to provide a unified Left version of 'culture' (out of the literary) and 'history' (out of the eponymous discipline). In his essay 'The poverty of theory', published in 1976, Thompson describes his own commitment to historical materialism, and he does so as part of that continuing debate which inveighs against the 'structuralist dalek', Althusser, and his ideological types in *New Left Review*. And because his quarrel is still the on-going sense of exclusion from abstract continental theory, the aspect of 'history' which he chooses to stress is that which is concerned with 'values', 'feelings', and 'morality' (the very history which abuts on the 'literary' – the Great Tradition, even). As Williams sees history as the missing element to be added to his early version of culture, so Thompson, in a critique which is represented as being about the importance of history, sees Althusser as incapable of handling culture:

> In the moment when we seem to be poised for further advances, we have been suddenly struck from the rear – and not from a rear of manifest 'bourgeois ideology' but from a rear claiming to be more Marxist than Marx. From the quarter of Louis Althusser and his numerous followers there has been launched an unmeasured assault upon 'historicism'. The advances of historical materialism, its supposed 'knowledge', have rested – it turns out – upon one slender and rotten epistemological pillar ('empiricism'); when Althusser submitted this pillar to a stern interrogation, it shuddered and crumbled to dust; and the whole enterprise of historical materialism collapsed in ruins around it. Not only does it turn out that men have never 'made their own history' at all . . . but it is also revealed that the enterprise of historical materialism . . . has been misbegotten from the start, since 'real' history is unknowable and cannot be said to exist.[33]

And again, but here explicitly linking (albeit by a 'ladies' hyphen) those 'values' lost from an Althusserian account with a peculiarly English 'political theory': 'Althusser (and his progeny) find themselves unable to handle, except in a most abstract and theoretic way, questions of value, culture – and political theory.'[34]

Williams had been explicit about what he needed from Thompson – the historical knowledge. Thompson is less explicit about a need from Williams, but in some ways, we shall argue, his is the greater dependency. What Thompson needs from Williams, and it becomes clear in the very critique he makes of Williams's *The Long Revolution*, is a particularly *literary* narrative, which can give agency to the characters of history, a narrative which is not the conventional one of the liberal historian, but one which can activate the categories of class and socialism.

Raymond Williams's recovery of an 'alternative' tradition gives the illusion to the historian that he has discovered new agents in the making of history. And Thompson presents us with new agents (without ever feeling the need to theorize them), to support that explicit 'making' of English socialism, and above all the English working class, which is the lynch-pin of his version of history (but which was also the object of insistent theoretical attack from his opponents). It is the authentic experience of the newly discovered agent, socialist man, which provides the momentum of his radical history. Unfortunately for Thompson, though, Raymond Williams's 'alternative' voice was oppositional within the acknowledged limitations of literary criticism. Thompson could only afford to acknowledge his own saturation in the English 'literary' if he could understand it as a political history. To acknowledge the relevance of Williams's *Culture and Society* to *himself* (the historian), Thompson needed to recognize his own dependency on English culture, and the voices it produced. As we saw in the previous chapter, Thompson did nothing of the sort; as a historian, he found in early Williams a set of middle-class voices, constructing culturally persuasive versions of class experience. And, as we again saw, he looked to the more avowedly historical (and political) *The Long Revolution* for a more direct personalizing of the class struggle. The unease is readily felt in passage after passage from that key review of Williams by Thompson: 'Oh, the sunlit quadrangle, the clinking of glasses of port, the quiet converse of enlightened men!'[35]

The 'central ambiguity' of the book, for Thompson, is that it never commits itself, either to history as something which 'happened like that', or, which men actively made. He appeals to Raymond Williams to show the lives of the 'common people' as active agents in the making of history, but the appeal is already revealing, citing a literary reference, the common people already constructed: 'And Jude and Sue in their lodgings across the way, which have now been "built into" our way of life. And what about *their* way of life, the way of the common people? Is it not relevant that they also had opinions . . .?'[36] We might ask who the 'our' is here. Is Thompson one of the 'common people' whose 'way of life' has assimilated the experience of Jude and Sue? Jude and Sue have been 'built into' '*our* way of life', but the way of the common people is '*their* way of life'. Are Jude and Sue ours or theirs? Is E. P. Thompson ours or theirs? And what is the status of that experience taken not from the life, but from the fiction? Thompson shows in his striving to build history around 'experience' a passion for Jude and Sue, a passion for literature which shows him deep in that version of culture which Williams is striving to problematize. Thompson 'lifts' the experience of Jude and Sue and turns it into a direct expression of class-consciousness, a constituent in the making of history. Williams, 'deficient' in history, knows that it cannot be that simple, and that our considerations of Jude and Sue have to be informed by the realization that they are textual, they are authored. And where is E. P. Thompson, in the 'our' or 'their' of the author, Thomas Hardy?

Thompson's classic review of Williams's *The Long Revolution* was published in two parts in consecutive issues of *New Left Review*. His wrestling with 'tone' and with Jude and Sue takes place in the first 'part' of the review. That part closes with an attempt on Thompson's part to pin down Williams's version of 'culture', in relation to his own 'history':

> We might note a tentative definition [of 'culture'] from the archaeologist, Professor Grahame Clark:
> 'Culture . . . may be defined as the measure of man's control over nature, a control exercised through experience among social groups and accumulated through the ages.'
> I do not offer this as a final definition: it is formulated in reply to different questions. But it seems to me to have two merits which are not to be found in the amateur tradition. First, it is a definition in terms of *function*: it raises the question of what culture *does* (or fails to do). Second, it introduces the notion of

culture as experience which has been 'handled' in specifically human ways, and so avoids the life equals way-of-life tautology. Any theory of culture must include the concept of the dialectical interaction between culture and something which is *not* culture. We must suppose the raw material of life-experience to be at one pole, and all the infinitely complex human disciplines and systems, articulate and inarticulate, formalised in institutions or dispersed in the least formal ways, which 'handle', transmit, or distort this raw material to be at the other. It is the active *process* – which is at the same time *the process through which men make their history* – that I am insisting upon: I would not dare, in this time of linguistic hypertension, to offer a new definition. What matters, in the end, is that the definition will help us to understand the processes of social change.[37]

The second part of the review wrestles with the whole notion of 'culture' as produced by Williams in *Culture and Society* and developed (or so Thompson maintains) in *The Long Revolution*.[38]

In the passage just quoted, Thompson attempts his definition of 'culture' in response to a felt need to *distinguish* Williams's 'cultural history' from his own 'history'. The debate occurs around Williams's use of the phrase 'the whole way of life': 'I see this cultural history as more than a department, a special area of change. In this creative area the changes and conflicts of the whole way of life are necessarily involved.'[39] Thompson rightly sees this as a special claim for culture in understanding the entirety of experience: 'If Williams by "the whole way of life" really means the *whole* way of life he is making a claim, not for cultural history, but for history.'[40]

But for Thompson there is always a 'raw material' of experience which lies outside culture, and provides the evidence for 'history'. In other words, whilst recognizing the introduction of 'culture' as Williams' significant contribution to Left thought, Thompson is reluctant to accept its consequences for history: 'If way of life equals culture then what is society apart from way of life: does society equal culture also?'[41] And in that case, does culture equal history? Worse still, does it send history down one of those branch-lines to be axed by Dr Beeching: 'making whole history schools into a kind of piece-meal baggage-train serving more ambitious departments'?[42]

In 1961, E. P. Thompson claims that Williams's inclusive version of cultural history has been taken up by *New Left Review* to justify an editorial policy which has attached too much significance to developments in literary and critical theory, as the crucial area of development of political theory, and not enough to the 'raw material' of working-class experience:

> [Mr Williams] is in command of the field and deserves to be so. But I am concerned at the fact that in the past few years so much stimulating writing has burgeoned in the field of criticism and of literary-sociology: so little in the sciences and in traditional social studies: and so very little in the field of political theory.
>
> But a problem of synthesis remains: these new areas of concern must be related in new ways with other areas of experience which are part of the working people's daily 'way of conflict'. Wages, after all, are for the millions very much a matter affecting the 'whole way of life', but for some time New Left Review has overlooked the point.[43]

This is at once revealing, in the context of our current discussion, and curious. At the very moment when Thompson acknowledges a powerful need for culture in his account of history (and praises Williams for providing it) he resists the implication in Williams's work that access to a 'whole way of life' is via analysis of culture, on the grounds that this produces a decadent view of politics as a collection of fragmentary academic specialisms (criticism, literary sociology), substituting for 'life' itself (whatever that Leavisite term implies) or the 'hard drudgery' of grass-roots Labour activists. New Left Review – the journal? the members of the editorial board? – stands, for Thompson, for this development in New Left thinking, and Williams is, for Thompson, a part of New Left Review (the journal, not the board). Thompson (by contrast) wants to theorize the raw material of working-class experience as history and narrate it as culture (narrate the way of life as a way of conflict).

Thompson seems to want to represent himself as somehow outside New Left Review (albeit writing in it), addressing a New Left movement, of which Williams is the figurehead and leading light, which is drifting away from authentic Marxist thought (Thompson on the margins), and towards elitism and intellectualism. What is curious is that it is difficult to detect any particularly strong commitment to Raymond Williams, of the kind Thompson indicates, in the pages of New Left Review itself. Indeed, even Thompson's confident opening assertion that 'within two months of the publication of The Long

Revolution the reception of the book is so well assured that I am released from the usual inhibitions upon a socialist reviewer – the need to repair the hostility of the general press', turns out to be completely at odds with Raymond Williams's own version of events:

> *NLR*: Are we right in recollecting that *The Long Revolution* got a much more inimical reception from the established press (than [*Culture and Society*]?

> The degree of hostility was quite unforgettable. There was a full-scale attack of the most bitter kind in certain key organs. The *TLS* was particularly violent and *ad hominem*. But the reaction was very general.

> *NLR*: What were your feelings on reading the long essay on the book written by Edward Thompson which appeared in *New Left Review* at the time? Was that the first extended critical notice you had received from the left?

> I think it probably was – in print at any rate. The whole nature of the culture at the time was such that fierce arguments and debates occurred all the time informally. One of the difficulties I had in focussing Edward's critique, as I told him, was that at the time I was under intense attack from the right: it really was extremely difficult to know in which direction to look. The onslaught from the right was so strong that I felt at certain moments an inability on the left to sustain theoretical differences and yet present a common front.[44]

So much for the 'assured' positive reception of *The Long Revolution* and the 'authority' of his work, 'which commands the respect of his opponents', to which Thompson refers.[45] In other words, in 1961 Thompson is already somehow recasting Williams, and particularly Williams's doctrine that access to class-consciousness is via the analysis of culture, as the theoretical 'centre' to his 'margin', and designating *New Left Review* editorial policy as the perpetrator of a Left theory which is supplanting authentic political theory.

This fictitious version of New Left alignments corresponds to Thompson's intellectual map at the time, rather than to the map of English Left politics. The questions Thompson asks of Hardy's Jude in the quotation with which we began this section are questions entirely typical of Thompson's approach to history (and via history, politics) in 1961, the approach given 'authority' in his 1955 book on William Morris. *William Morris*, as we shall see in the next chapter, is the narrative account. Theoretically stringent answers to any of these questions will inevitably be derived from the domain of the cultural (including the literary) – the domain which Thompson absorbs but does not acknowledge, which Williams explicitly addresses, and which Thompson, in 1961, feels he is somehow 'on the edge' of, excluded somehow (and somehow blaming that exclusion already on *New Left Review*) from the requisite expertise, marginalized by Williamsite cultural theory.

Thompson had seen that the directions which *New Left Review* was taking effectively marginalized his own historical approach. The appointment of Perry Anderson as editor in early 1962, and the journal's publishing policy thereafter, gradually confirmed this. By 1964 it seems that E. P. Thompson had every right to feel aggrieved at the ability of contributors to respond fully to Williams whilst apparently overlooking *him*. *The Making of the English Working Class* was published in 1963; in 1964 Anderson's broadside against English socialism and the failure of the Labour movement, 'Origins of the present crisis' – an article which focused on Marxist history as that area most strikingly deficient in theorizing Britain's twentieth-century political decline – glaringly fails to register (perhaps even to have read) *The Making of the English Working Class*.[46]

It was not as if E. P. Thompson was not acknowledged to be a leading Marxist historian. Even in Anderson, 'marxist historians, whose mature works are only now beginning to emerge and consolidate each other'[47] must surely include Thompson. However, either deliberately or inadvertently, Anderson treats Thompson's vast attempt at a materialist history of the English working class as a piece of English 'cultural provincialism', to the point of excluding it altogether from his account (where even Hoggart gets a mention).[48] It would have been insulting enough to Thompson had Anderson chosen to give a negative critique of Thompson's version of the history of the working class. To ignore its political significance altogether was to bundle it in with other pieces of parochial and academic historical writing from the Left, as part of 'the nervelessness of [English] historiography':

We must be unique among advanced industrial nations in having *not one single structural* study of our society today; but this stupefying absence follows logically from the complete lack of any serious global history of British society in the 20th century. The limits of our sociology reflect the nervelessness of our historiography. Marxist historians, whose mature works are only now beginning to emerge and consolidate each other, have so far nearly all confined themselves to the heroic periods of English history, the 17th and early 19th centuries: most of the 18th and all of the 20th remain unexplored. Thus no attempt has ever been made at even the outline of a 'totalizing' history of modern British society. Yet until our view of Britain today is grounded in some vision of its full, effective past, however misconceived and transient this may initially be, we will continue to lack the basis for any understanding of the dialectical movements of our society, and hence – necessarily – of the contradictory possibilities within it which alone can yield a strategy for socialism.[49]

No wonder Thompson was enraged – not even to be allowed into the discussion as 'misconceived and transient'.

In 1965 (apparently a lapse of two years of stifled outrage, but actually prompted by the reprinting of 'Origins' in *Towards Socialism*) pointedly outside *New Left Review* itself, in *Socialist Register*, which favoured intellectual debate more immediately relevant to the Labour Party, Thompson replied to the implicit insult of 'Origins' with 'The peculiarities of the English' (even taking his title from Anderson: 'This peculiarity of the English political system must, again, be referred to the historical evolution of the ruling bloc').[50] Nairn's 'Anatomy of the Labour Party', published in *NLR* 27 and 28 explicitly as a pragmatic discussion of the state of the Labour Party derived from Anderson's theoretical position, provided Thompson with the excuse for engaging with Anderson and Nairn in the terms of *Socialist Register*.[51] Though Anderson had himself, on the issue of class, already laid himself on the line:

In Britain, the working class has generated over 150 years a massive adamantive [*sic*] class-consciousness – but it has never developed into a hegemonic political force. The very name of its traditional political party poignantly underlines this truth. Alone of major European working-class parties, it is called neither a Social-Democratic party nor a Socialist nor a Communist Party; it is the *Labour* Party – the name designates, not an ideal society, as do all the others, but simply an existent interest.[52]

The consistent disparaging by both Anderson and Nairn of the
English working class as mindless recipients of a set of bourgeois
attitudes – 'complacent confusion of influence with power, bovine
admiration for bureaucracy, ill-conceived contempt for equality,
bottomless philistinism' ('a proletariat distinguished by *an immovable
corporate class-consciousness and almost no hegemonic ideology*') –
allowed Thompson to set himself up in 'Peculiarities' as Marxist
champion of the working class.[53] And in the ensuing vituperative
debate it became imperative for Anderson to justify his original
omission of Thompson (an error, and probably a serious error of
judgement) on the grounds that Thompson's version of 'agency' in
that deliberately punning 'making' of the English working class, was
hopelessly confused:

> In other words, the tacit first version of experience to be found
> in *The Poverty of Theory* – a set of mental and emotional
> responses as it were 'given with' a set of lived events to which
> they correspond – cannot be sustained. However, as we have
> seen, Thompson also sketches a second definition, which seems to
> allow for divergences and variations of response much better.
> Here, experience itself remains an objective sector of 'social
> being', which is then processed or handled by the subject to yield
> a particular 'social consciousness'. The possibility of different
> ways of 'handling' the same experience is epistemologically
> secured. This schema represents, in fact, the more recurrent and
> important of the two accounts advanced by Thompson, although
> there is a significant degree of oscillation between them. To see
> it worked through on a grand scale, we must turn to *The Making
> of the English Working Class*. In doing so, we will immediately
> rejoin the problem of historical agency at the deepest levels of
> Thompson's intellectual engagement with it. This great work
> opens with the famous declaration: 'The working class did not rise
> like the sun at an appointed time. It was present at its own
> making'. For this making was an active process, 'which owes as
> much to agency as to conditioning'. The early English proletariat
> was not the mere product of the advent of the factory system. On
> the contrary, 'the working class made itself as much as it was
> made'. The fundamental form this agency took was the conversion
> of a collective experience into a social consciousness which
> thereby defined and created the class itself.[54]

Ironically, by 1980, when Anderson wrote this in *Arguments Within*

English Marxism, the argument was in fact over. *The Making of the English Working Class* was simply no longer vulnerable to charges of 'slipping' between cultural and immediate versions of experience, because it had itself become the model for an acceptable type of historical account of class and agency in history. And at this stage (in 1980) Anderson's preoccupation with Thompson's 1963 (by now) classic work has the curious effect of lionizing him, in the very act of 'brilliantly' exposing the flaws in his argument. In itself, we are bound today to find this account less interesting than his earlier ones, because it is clear with hindsight that Anderson is here over-compensating for having originally underestimated the effect of Thompson on the Labour movement. And this tends to distract from the disturbingly contradictory models of class that we have here – contradictions which are busily being swept under the carpet in the interests of a coherent account of English Marxism consistent both with Williams and with Thompson. Anderson has become, belatedly, the honest broker between them, and in taking on this role, relinquishes his crucial one as the only Marxist historian intervening in the debate in such a way as to make prominent the *difficulties* inherent in such an attempt at reconciliation.

It is no accident that in Anderson's later account of agency in Thompson, the term 'culture' is missing except as a sign of weakness ('It would not be just to call this declaration "cultural nationalism", but it may readily be seen that in irascible mood – unfortunately not infrequent since the mid 60s – the same sensibility can become aggressively nationalist: *in culture*').[55] Yet 'culture' is the link-term between *Culture and Society* and *The Making of the English Working Class*, and between *The Long Revolution* and *William Morris*, which by 1980 has synthesized Williams ('*Culture and Society* and *The Long Revolution* undoubtedly represent the major contribution to socialist thought in England since the war')[56] and Thompson ('English marxism')[57] to provide a peculiarly English Left historical methodology. It is a methodology designed to explicate the problems inherent in the kinds of classic formulations of class and agency in English history which are to be found in *The Making of the English Working Class*:

> More than this, the notion of class entails the notion of historical relationship. Like any other relationship, it is a fluency which evades analysis if we attempt to stop it dead at any given moment

and anatomize its structure. . . . Class happens when some men, as a result of common experiences (inherited or shared), feel and articulate the identity of their interests as between themselves, and as against other men whose interests are different from (and usually opposed to) theirs. The class experience is largely determined by the productive relations into which men are born – or enter involuntarily. Class-consciousness is the way in which the experiences are handled in cultural terms: embodied in traditions, value-systems, ideas and institutional forms.[58]

Or again, a page later:

The question, of course, is how the individual got to be in this 'social role', and how the particular social organisation (with its property rights and structure of authority) got to be there. And these are historical questions. If we stop history at a given point, then there are no classes, but simply a multitude of individuals with a multitude of experiences. But if we watch these men over an adequate period of social change, we observe patterns in their relationships, their ideas, and their institutions. Class is defined by men as they live their own history, and, in the end, this is its only definition.[59]

Yet in the context of the present discussion, quotations such as this clearly *require* the use of the term 'culture' for their explication. But as the crucially problematic term in the Williams/Thompson liaison, it is also the term Anderson seems now particularly to want to avoid.

It is additionally significant that Anderson should choose to address his critique of Thompson on 'agency' as the focus of his chapter on *The Making of the English Working Class*, in *Arguments Within English Marxism* (which, remember, is a chapter-by-chapter critique of each of Thompson's published works). Anderson's most anodyne (later) chapter is the chapter entitled 'Utopia', which deals with the earlier (1955) work, *William Morris*. Yet it is *William Morris*, which Anderson is prepared to take on board as a classic account of the origins of English socialism, which first raises for Thompson all those problems of historical methodology which he finally resolves via Williams and (inadvertently) the literary. In Thompson's most vivid, retrospective account of his own involvement with Morris he makes it explicit that it was in *this* work that he first felt the intolerable tensions between conventional Marxist history and his own Left historical approach:

> If I write about Morris again it will be in my character, not as historian, but as socialist. For I must set one misunderstanding at rest. It might seem that, in the revaluation proposed in this Postscript, I have been setting myself up as yet one more 'claimant' of Morris, in the attempt to attach him to an idiosyncratic Thompsonian position. But the case is the reverse. Morris, by 1955, had claimed me. My book was then, I suppose, already a work of muffled 'revisionism'. The Morris/Marx argument has worked inside me ever since. When, in 1956, my disagreements with orthodox Marxism became fully articulate, I fell back on modes of perception which I had learned in those years of close company with Morris, and I found, perhaps, the will to go on arguing from the pressure of Morris behind me. To say that Morris claimed me, and that I have tried to acknowledge that claim, gives me no right to claim him. I have no licence to act as his interpreter. But at least I can now say that this is what I have been trying, for twenty years, to do.[60]

And it is, surely, Thompson's sense of Morris as some kind of crux in his own Left thinking which makes him urgently say: 'We have to make up our minds about William Morris.'[61]

If we read back from Thompson's separation of the historian and the socialist here, the 'we' of 'we have to make up our minds about William Morris' can only be historians or readers of history. But Morris has also, literally, 'made up the author's mind' already, Morris has 'worked inside [him]', he has been formed by the 'pressure of Morris behind [him]'. And that 'having been claimed by' Morris has produced Thompson, twenty years later, as *socialist* – who will only write again on Morris in his (Thompson's) character *as* a socialist – after twenty years of writing as historian.

The question however remains. *Why* do we (whoever we are) have to make up our minds about Morris? And the answer, of course, is: because 'radical theory' has been marked, in its developments since the late 1950s, by arguments about history, culture, and class-consciousness which are unmistakably shaped by Thompson's so-called 'historian's' version of Morris. (And we shall inevitably argue that that in itself compromises the position of women within that 'radical theory'.) Pragmatically that is evidenced in the repeated invoking of Morris in (for example) *Marxism Today* in ways in which Shaw, Tawney, or Robert Owen are not. Morris has been invoked, in Thompson's words, as an 'alternative notation of value': an alternative, that is, for the English Left, to their equally bearded hero of the European movement, Marx, and an alternative who carries a particular configuration of English class politics in the relationships we mention – those of history, culture, and class-consciousness. Morris has been circulated for two decades as the English socialist figure we ought most to be dealing with academically (quarried of information and 'worked surreptiously for doctoral advancement'), and as the figure best able to represent a socialist vision characterized by three central elements or drives: romanticism, moralism, and utopianism.

But this leaves one further question. In this case, why do *we* have to make up our minds about William Morris *as women* on the Left? We might ask again (as in the last chapter): 'What has it to do with us?'.[62] We have indicated in this chapter that interwoven with the struggles between old and new guards of the male New Left there runs the thread of rejection and exclusion of women from that entire debate – that drowning out of Juliet Mitchell and her seminal (for the women's movement) 'Women: *The Longest Revolution*'. So that there appears to be a strong sense in which, in the developing of a coherent approach on the male Left to history and culture, the questions which concerned women on the Left were not put, or if put (by the women), not heard as part of the debate. We shall have to re-excavate that historical moment at which Mitchell voiced the questions for women on the Left, but was shouted down, since this turns out to have profound consequences for the Labour movement.

Chapter Three

Writing history with a vengeance
Getting good Marx with William Morris (and Jane's Burden)

The Marxist tradition can and should be criticized for its failure to understand the specificity of women. Juliet Mitchell's instinct is correct here, but since she does not define the specificity in socio-economic terms she falls into simple empirical description. The Marxist tradition can be criticized in particular for its mistaken identification of the social role of women, in treating them as if they were a class; for workers or peasants are exploited actively, at their place of work, while women's subordination is a passive one – they are appropriated together with other property. The central weakness of her whole analysis is that she bases it on ahistorical categories: fundamental, marginal, etc.

Her own article is, in fact, itself an unwitting proof that it is impossible to achieve a global analysis of the position of women *outside* the premises of classical Marxist discussion. For her discussion too moves from the family (sexuality, socialization, and reproduction) to productive work. Failing to situate women historically, in socio-economic terms, her position remains the traditional feminist one, which is in its essence moralistic: the history of women is presented as a sequence of oppression by the male sex. . . .

The family used to be an economic unit – today it is not. On the basis of this, she suggests that the idea of the family being a form of private property is incorrect today. Because she does not understand the concept in the writings of Marx and Engels, she equates no family with a state of common property – and uses a quotation from Marx incorrectly to make the point. She does not see, therefore, that merely to replace monogamy by a plurality of marriages is to retain private property relations in the future socialist society. . . . Juliet Mitchell never admits that the family is a form of private property.

(Quintin Hoare)[1]

47

Quintin Hoare criticises me for 'never admitting that the family is a form of private property'. I don't admit it, because I don't think it is. It is a *means* for the retention and attainment of private property and so is the woman within it. But not unless women are literally exchange products can they be *identical* with objects and property. Industrialism *does* separate the family from its earlier immediate associations with the economy and this separation prevents in any case the total coincidence of the family and private property. It seems that Quintin Hoare is asking us to analyse the position of women in pre-industrial conditions. Elsewhere he confirms this preoccupation: '. . . the "economist" approach of Marx and Engels is *the basis* for a discussion of the position of women. What specifies the position of women in history *until the industrial revolution* (my italics) is that her participation in production is mediated through the family'. To concentrate on this pre-industrial area – even assuming the hypothesis is correct – would be to write history with a vengeance.

(Juliet Mitchell)[2]

1984 was not just Orwell's year: it was the 150th anniversary of the birth of William Morris. *Marxism Today* marked that milestone anniversary in the 'history' of English Marxism with a tribute to 'a neglected figure', but one whose 'preoccupations can offer the Left much in its present predicament' (that predicament of Orwellian technological tyranny and moral decline):

Morris's originality as a Marxist rests on the encounter in his mind between literary and aesthetic concerns, and criticisms Victorian society expressed through them, and the works of Marx. It is not simply that this enables Morris to 'add on' ethical and cultural dimensions absent in Marx. Rather, Morris reads Marx in a way that can expand our understanding of 'material production' and social relations. For Morris production always involves the reproduction of a whole culture, sets of values and forms of social relationship, not just the sphere of 'economic' life narrowly understood. His concern with 'how we live and how we might live' (the title of one of Morris's best-known lectures) leads him to question the aspirations and goals of the socialist movement.[3]

The first question we are prompted to ask is, *is* this an account of how Morris read Marx? It is certainly an account, of an appropriately celebratory kind, of how, by 1984, English Marxism reads Morris – reads Morris to make good Marx, or Marx to make good

Morris. And we know that we don't have far to look for the origin of such a reading. E. P. Thompson defined its terms in 1955, at the time of his falling out with 'orthodox marxism' – when he 'fell back on modes of perception which [he] had learned in those years of close company with Morris':

> What was the source of the greatness of Morris – this growing stature which he assumes in the perspective of history? . . . Did he make any major contribution which is marked by the stamp of unquestionable originality and excellence?
> The answer must be, 'Yes'. Morris's claim to greatness must be founded, not by any single contribution to English culture, but on the quality which unites and informs every aspect of his life and work. This quality might best be described as 'moral realism': it is the practical moral example of his life which wins admiration, the profound moral insight of his political and artistic writings which gives them life.[4]

It is this 'moral realism' which enables *Thompson* to '"add on" ethical and cultural dimensions absent in Marx'. It is Thompson who 'reads Marx in a way that can expand our understanding of "material production" and social relations'. E. P. Thompson's *William Morris*, far from leaving Morris a neglected figure, has, by 1984, installed his biography as the 'making of socialism' quite as securely as the later work of Thompson's installed his account of early nineteenth-century political movements as the 'making of the English working class'.[5]

By 1980, actually. In 1980, Perry Anderson publicly confessed to having underestimated the importance of Thompson's early work on Morris:

> There is no doubt that the cadet group [*sic*] which remodelled *NLR* in 1964–1965 entirely failed to register the significance of Thompson's first major book [*William Morris*]. This can be seen most obviously in its denial of any important Marxist past in England – a wilful way of overlooking Morris, whose genius Thompson had declared to be 'peculiarly English'; but most essentially in its insensitivity to the major claim for Morris's greatness entered by Thompson – his 'moral realism': not only the 'practical moral example of his life' and the 'profound moral insight of his political and artistic writings', but 'the appeal to the moral consciousness as a vital agency of social change'. This claim is

convincingly substantiated by Thompson's study. Today its qualities have probably achieved duly wide acknowledgement for the first time, with the reissue of the book in its revised edition. The *Postscript* with which it now ends, surveying the literature on Morris in the intervening twenty years, must be accounted one of Thompson's most important political and theoretical statements in its own right. It reintroduces Morris directly into the quick of contemporary socialist debate by laying special stress on the nature and stature of his utopianism.[6]

Readers of the last chapter will not have difficulty in recognizing that it was not William Morris, but E. P. Thompson, who *NLR* had overlooked. They had 'failed to register the significance of Thompson's first major book' – the book, not the nineteenth-century artist and socialist, had been neglected, had failed to find a place in that formative 1960s account of those 'peculiarities' of English Marxism which for Anderson and Nairn were responsible for the 'origins of the present crisis'. When they did discover Thompson the biographer (as opposed to Thompson the tiresome member of the 'Old Guard' on *NLR*) the shock of the discovery was that of recognition of their own place in (by then) English Marxism. And it is the *particularity* of Thompson's biographical account of Morris (a particularity on which we shall dwell for most of this chapter) which means that since they can recognize 'Morris, father of English marxism' only in Thompson's version (rather than, say, in Mackail's or Lindsay's),[7] they are forced to draw the conclusion that the *important* Morris continues to be 'neglected' apart from that account.

So, we need to ask what it is which distinguishes Thompson's Morris from the Morris of all the other biographers? The most readily available answer comes from the early reviews, as quoted by Thompson in his 1976 'Postscript': what distinguished it at first was its overt Marxism – delivered in a tone judged 'splenetic' by critical reviewers.[8] But that is curiously not an answer which will satisfy a reader in the 1980s. In the 1980s that Marxist spleen seems difficult to detect, and that is worth noting. In 1955 it was Marxist enough to show over 900 pages of biography that a respectable canonical writer/artist was by political conviction a committed follower of Marx. But by 1976, Thompson distinguishes *his* biography not only from 'anti-marxist' bandwaggoners on the Morris revival train, but most insistently from subsequent biographies which claim Morris as an orthodox Marxist: 'The important question might be not whether

Morris was or was not a Marxist, but whether he was a Morrisist.'[9] And again: 'We can now see that Morris may be assimilated to Marxism only in the process of self-criticism and re-ordering within Marxism itself'.[10]

In other words, by 1976, Thompson can maintain that there is no point in aligning Morris with orthodox Marxism any longer, and that it is the very poorness of the fit between any account that can be given of 'Morrisism' and 'Marxism' which (since by now Morris is indubitably *some* kind of Marxist) makes 'Morrisism' the crucial English version of Marx. Effectively the 'Postscript' is a self-conscious testimony (in its itemizing of the numerous 'derivative' biographies published in the twenty years since Thompson's *William Morris*'s first appearance) to the now authoritative position of that account of William Morris as the acceptable (bearded) English face of the political Marxist.[11] And this is no overestimation. Because what Thompson, the author of *The Making of the English Working Class*, can see by 1976, is that *William Morris* (what Thompson has made of Morris) has authorized a particular moralizing/Morrisizing bent in English radical history.

We can see most clearly what this moralizing bent consists of (what its concealed premises might be, and what its less considered implications) in Thompson's retrospective 'Postscript'. What we see peculiarly vividly in the context of the present exploration is that the 1955 view of Morris/Marx which Thompson re-authorizes in 1976 is validated in terms recognizably derived from Williams's *Culture and Society* (which had been published, we remember, three years *after* the publication of *William Morris*).[12] By 1976 Thompson writes, as his final verdict on Morris (if he writes about him again, it will be 'as a socialist'): 'We may see in William Morris, not a late Victorian, nor even a "contemporary", but a new kind of sensibility.'[13] This comes directly from the chapter on 'Marxism and Culture', in which Williams discusses at length the importance of Romanticism for Marxists, as does Thompson's concluding account of Morris's commitment to a 'whole alternative way of life'. This is not something that Thompson tries in any way to conceal. Quite the contrary; since this is also the chapter in which (as Thompson reminds us) Williams includes some discussion of Thompson's *William Morris* itself:[14]

I may seem to be dancing on the point of a pin [morris dancing?], but others have danced there before me. Raymond Williams, when offering in 1958 a cogent criticism of the self-contradictions of English Marxist critics (including myself) noted: 'It certainly seems relevant to ask English Marxists who have interested themselves in the arts whether this is not Romanticism absorbing Marx, rather than Marx transforming Romanticism. It is a matter of opinion which one would prefer to happen.' (274)

But, if we let Morris stand in for 'Romanticism', these are not the only alternatives. It is possible also to envisage the Romantic tradition, transformed as it was by Morris (in part through his encounter with Marx), entering into a common Communist tradition to which it could contribute its particular emphases, vocabulary and concerns. It was a distinctive contribution of *Culture and Society* to show how tough this long Romantic critique of industrial capitalism had been; and I would add that Williams's own writing, over two decades, has exemplified how tough a mutation of that tradition can still be, and how congruent to the thought of Marx.[15]

There is, however, clearly something wrong with this claim of Thompson's that his work is crucially related to Williams's ('It is of interest that I and Raymond Williams, whose important *Culture and Society* appeared three years after this book, should have been, unknown to each other, working upon different aspects of the Romantic critique of Utilitarianism' (769)). What strikes us is how insistently Thompson's choice of 'critical' terminology, purportedly that of Williams (which Thompson acknowledges, in full confidence that Williams's own Marxism therefore confirms his own terminology *as* Marxist) nevertheless recalls Leavis to anyone schooled in literary criticism. That is to say, the very fact that Thompson does *not* himself know that tradition (why should he?) deprives him of the possibility of seeing how Williams had had to distinguish his own 'oppositional' account of culture very carefully from that of Leavis – from a traditional, and ultimately reactionary, liberal humanism.

Thompson does not see the problem (nor, we shall show, do other historians, shielded like him from the lit. crit. heritage). More than that, in 1976 he chooses to overlook problems he *had* seen in Williams's 'cultural' history fifteen years earlier, problems raised specifically by a certain lack of precision in Williams as to whether his oppositional culture was to be taken as continuous with, or discontinuous from traditional culture. When Thompson deals with

Stanley Pierson's *Marxism and the Origins of British Socialism* (London, 1973) in the Morris 'Postscript' he asserts that there is necessarily a rupture between Morris's 'sensibility' and that of 'the Victorians' – a rupture which establishes Morris as both potentially and actually revolutionary. In that 1961 *NLR* review of Williams's *The Long Revolution*, Thompson had expressed anxiety about the notion (implicit, in his view in Williams's work) that revolution can be accomplished by continuous development and assimilation; in the 'Postscript' he is at pains (on his own behalf) to explain that his account of William Morris is consistent with a theory that late nineteenth-century socialism formed a distinct break – a rupture – with Victorian liberalism:

> Very sharp theoretical confrontations were taking place, in which emergent Socialist thought contested with the 'common-sense' of Victorian liberal-capitalist society and its dominant ideological illusions. And the reminder leads us to two attendant considerations. First, in what sense did the new Socialist theory (and its strategies) constitute a critical break, or rupture, not with this or that point of liberal Victorian thought, but with the organising ideas of bourgeois Liberalism? If we argue that it did constitute such a rupture, it need not follow that the new Socialist theory was in all respects mature, coherent and without self-contradiction; it follows only that at critical points, and in certain controlling ideas, this theory was antagonistic to bourgeois ideology, and, specifically, proposed not the amelioration of the liberal capitalist state, but its revolutionary transformation. . . .
>
> I'm not suggesting that there are some talismanic concepts (Marx's theory of value, the theory of the State) which allow us instantly to identify whether the controlling theory of any personal group is 'bourgeois' or 'revolutionary'. Analysis will never be as easy as that. Still less am I suggesting that there is one single, 'correct', immanent Socialist orthodoxy. I'm arguing, as I argued twenty-one years ago, that there *is* a 'river of fire'.[16]

That 'critical break, or rupture, not with this or that point of liberal Victorian thought, but with the organizing ideas of bourgeois Liberalism' is what Raymond Williams claims as the organizing assumption behind his reassessment of (his discovery of a submerged, alternative tradition in) late-nineteenth-century culture, in *Culture and Society*, and, like Thompson, he sees the break as 'absolutely crucial', above all for Marxism:

The origins of the book lie in ideas of either explicitly conservative or contradictory thinkers in the nineteenth century – but conservatives who, at the point of irruption of a qualitatively new social order put many of the right questions to it but of course came out with wrong answers.[17]

The thinking about the process of industrial transformation that was done in the period between Blake and Wordsworth and Southey and the young Carlyle, although it is very early and confused, still seems to me absolutely crucial. . . . Now this form of thought was not an element that a subsequent ampler tradition has sufficiently taken into account except in what are self-evidently reactionary ways. . . . It was [after the War] that the questions posed by Blake and Cobbett acquired their force for me. They had a sense of the materiality of production that was largely lost afterwards. . . . In those mixed English reactions to the industrial revolution was a response which it seems to me any Marxism in this part of the century would have to include.[18]

But what *makes* the break, for Williams, is his conscious sense of telling the story differently, recovering 'the true complexity of the tradition [reactionary thinking] had confiscated' (98): 'I knew perfectly well who I was writing against: Eliot, Leavis, and the whole of the cultural conservatism that had formed around them – the people who had pre-empted the culture and literature of this country.'[19] So that for Williams there are the faltering, provisional moves made by some Victorian thinkers, and there is the decisive, considered break which he, the critic, makes with the conservative critical tradition which has given a coherent, reactionary account of 'Victorian liberal-capitalist society and its dominant ideological illusions', in which any potential for 'rupture' is carefully erased.

Thompson's sense of 'rupture' is altogether more confident, and, moreover, placed squarely on the shoulders of Morris – his 'experience' of Victorian liberalism; his conscious dissociation from it, transcendence of it:

So there are two disagreements [with Pierson], and each of them is large. First, I hold, against Pierson, that certain critical and controlling Socialist concepts were not 'superimposed' upoon Morris's Romantic critique, but were indeed integrated with it, and in such a way as to constitute a rupture in the older tradition, and to signal its transformation. Insofar as these concepts were consonant with those of Marx, and were in some cases derived directly from Marxist sources, we ought to call them Marxist. Second, I hold, against Pierson, that the Romantic tradition is not to be defined only in terms of its traditional, conservative, 'regressive', 'escapist', and 'utopian' characteristics – and hence to be seen as a continual undertow threatening to draw Morris back to 'subjectivism' and 'idealism' – but contained within it resources of a quite different nature, capable of undergoing this transformation independently of the precipitate of Marx and Engels's writing. This is to say, the moral critique of capitalist process was pressing forward to conclusions consonant with Marx's critique, *and it was Morris's particular genius to think through this transformation, effect this juncture, and seal it with action.* [our italics] Nor should Pierson have been unaware that the typing of this Romantic critique as 'regressive', 'utopian', and 'idealist' is a facile way of getting out of the problem, for an alternative way of reading this tradition had been proposed, not only in this book, in 1955, but very cogently, by Raymond Williams in *Culture and Society* in 1958.[20]

Here Thompson gives us William Morris, popular hero, individualist agent of change. Raymond Williams finds no such simple heroic agency in his account of nineteenth-century culture. And *his* William Morris is 'diluted' by regressive elements from Ruskin, to the extent that the 'larger part of his literary work bears witness only to the disorder which he felt so acutely' (159):

> The transition to social criticism is then quite natural, within the forms of Ruskin's thinking. It is best understood, as I have indicated, in the context of a *general* transition between thinking about art and thinking about society: the transition which is marked, in all its complexity of reference, by the changes in the meanings of *culture*. The 'organic society', the 'whole way of life', and similar phrases, are certainly open to charges of obscurity, but they are not in any case likely to be understood except by reference to concepts of experience largely drawn from the practice and study of art, which are their basis and substance. We have seen how the idea of 'wholeness', as a distinguishing quality of the mind of the artist, led Ruskin into a criticism of society by the same criterion, which was in fact to be most influential.[21]

The regressive elements are present in Morris, as they were in

Ruskin. These elements seek to compensate for the difficulties in the way of practical realization of certain qualities of life; and because their function is compensatory, they are often sentimental. Yet, although their reference is to the past, their concern is with the present and the future. When we stress, in Morris, the attachment to handicrafts, we are, in part, rationalizing an uneasiness generated by the scale and nature of his social criticism.[22]

In other words, where the 'literary' generates Morris's ethically definitive Marxism for Thompson, it is, in the end, for Williams, the impediment to a unified politically aware Morris.

The key difference between Thompson's and Williams's Morris seems to hang on their assessment of the 'reference to the past' as a component in his thought. Thompson's persistent elision of 'art' with his crucial 'ethical' component in 'Morrisism' allows him confidently to produce Morris's medievalism *as* that 'way of life' which is to be substituted for the politically unacceptable present – which defines the ideal socialist 'sensibility'. But as Raymond Williams is aware, the medievalist and pre-industrial preoccupations of William Morris – his 'organic community' – may equally be harnessed to a conservative or to a progressive account of society:

> If Ruskin's criticisms of the nineteenth-century economy are examined piecemeal, he may at times be seen as a socialist forerunner – as indeed he has been often described. It is perhaps true that the ideas of an 'organic' society are an essential preparation for socialist theory, and for the more general attention to a 'whole way of life', in opposition to theories which consistently reduce social to individual questions, and which support legislation of an individualist as opposed to a collectivist kind. But the theories can hardly be abstracted from actual social situations, and the 'organic' theory has in fact been used in support of very different, and even opposing, causes.[23]

How damaging the uncritical version of medievalism is for socialism (let alone Marxism) can be seen in that *Marxism Today* celebration of Morris:

> Morris's interest in the Middle Ages likewise represented – *long before he became involved in socialist politics* [our italics] – the possibility of a radically different society. Whatever they meant for other middle class Victorians – including readers of his verse

– the Middle Ages meant for Morris the implicit hope that, since things had been different in the past, they might again be different in the future. This is much more than pure 'escapism'. Morris was a 'cultural materialist' long before his encounter with Marx. The medieval world he evokes in *The Earthly Paradise* 1868–70, his most widely read work among the 'respectable' reading public, is characterised by its variety, sensuousness and richness of colouring and texture.[24]

Nowhere in Thompson would you find such a straightforward endorsement of the utopian strand in Morris *as* 'cultural materialism'. Yet we would wish to stress that such a line of thought descends directly from Thompson, via his 'moral realism'.

'Realism', in the sense in which Thompson uses it, and his followers take it up, is part of that terminology which allows the critic to pass from art to experience – to produce art as that 'totality' which builds values into a (specified) account of experience.[25] *Moral* realism simply emphasizes that value-laden quality of the account – 'realism' allows you to put the moralizing in, and the explicitness of 'moral' entitles you to take it out again.[26] If this sounds like a rather brutal account of the issues involved, we would maintain that our argument up to this point in this chapter entitles us to present it in this way. In the intersection Williams/*Culture and Society* with Thompson/*William Morris* the aesthetic dimension which complicates Williams's engagement with 'values' is entirely suppressed. In 1955 Thompson was apparently unaware of his own literary formation. And when subsequently called to account, he dodges his own commitment to aestheticism (the domain from which 'realism' is taken), and whenever he finds himself confronted with it as part of his argument, he defers to Williams's *Culture and Society*.[27]

If we now return to our opening quotations from Hoare and Mitchell, we can see why that juxtaposition of the pre-industrial with the moralizing of the family is menacing. Mitchell's response to Hoare carries that fear – writing history with a vengeance – of what happens to women when the model of social relations is pre-industrial. What we are saying, with Mitchell, is that, in the pre-industrial model of social relations (which, as she points out, in the contemporary male Left account, may be, in itself, a set of mythologies), the family is moralized in ways which leave women in a particularly unradicalized position. Nothing shows this more clearly than that work about which the male Left continues to feel so wistfully nostalgic, Morris's *News From Nowhere*.

Where Hoare can see women only as objects – property for exchange – and not as workers, Mitchell is, in her turn, baffled by his inability to see women as political subjects. His conviction is that 'the whole *historical* development of women has been within the family. We may all agree that her place should not be there, but it is'. And as Mitchell sees, it is the pre-industrial which moralizes the family in history, and constrains women entirely within it. Mitchell digs her heels in against that invoking of 'pre-industrialism' because as a woman she can already *feel* how that trails the whole baggage of Thompson's Morrisism – feels it for the way in which it does confine available analysis of women's politics to a politics of the family.

News From Nowhere has been represented by the male Left as 'a triumphant resolution [of] all Morris's deepest inner conflicts',[28] or, at worst, as an innocent dream of a future, uncorrupted society ('the sweet little world at the end of all this at once a result and a promise').[29] As women readers, we have always found ourselves in a difficult position over these interpretations. On the one hand, it is hard to avoid a giggle at the saccharin delusions of the male mind, desiring serving wenches who fulfil all the ideal types of family life, ecstatic about housework and motherhood, and, also, of course aesthetically pleasing. On the other hand, we can hardly bear to quote these sections, knowing, at some level, that their configurations are obviously awful, whilst knowing that that fact does not strike the male Left reader as important, does not disturb his sense of the radicalism of the piece (as it does ours):[30]

Our breakfast was spread for us; and, as we sat down, one of them hurried out by the chambers aforesaid, and came back in a little while with a great bunch of roses, . . . she hurried back thence into the buttery, and came back once more with a delicately made glass, into which she put the flowers and set them down in the midst of our table. One of the others, who had run off also, then came back with a big cabbage-leaf filled with strawberries, some of them barely ripe. . . . One of the girls, the handsome one, who had been scattering little twigs of lavender and other sweet smelling herbs about the floor, came near to listen, and stood behind me with her hand on my shoulder, in which she held some of the plant that I used to call balm: its strong sweet smell brought back to my mind my very early days in the kitchen-garden at Woodford, and the large blue plums which grew on the wall beyond the sweet-herb patch – a connection of memories which all boys will see at once. . . . I stared at her, and drew musical laughter from her again; but I might well stare, for there was not a careful line on her face; her skin was as smooth as ivory, her cheeks full and round, her lips as red as the roses she had brought in; her beautiful arms, which she had bared for her work, firm and well-knit from shoulder to wrist.[31]

It is the culturedness of the narrative – its literariness, its aesthetics – which at once persuades the male Left reader that this is 'visionary politics', whilst allowing him to overlook its reactionary representation of gendered social relations. And it is the cultured narrative of E. P. Thompson which launches the same set of paradigms into our English version of contemporary socialism, with a moralizing of William Morris's wife-to-be, Jane Burden, the men's Janey, which shows that Morris's serving wenches in *News From Nowhere* have nothing to do with Morris being aberrant, nor with innocence, but are part of the narrative which allows Thompson's version of William Morris to happen *as* our socialist tradition (Marxism and moral realism).

The male Left's attachment to medievalism (or pre-industrialism) from Morris to Thompson to Hoare to *Marxism Today* is, as we have seen, an attachment which is quite independent of its attachment to explicit socialism. It is an attachment to that cultured narrative which is wilfully blind to its own history in high culture and English nationalism. The serving wenches in *News From Nowhere* are to us, as women readers, an indicator of this, but to the male Left reader they are presumably just pretty, an aesthetic, the decorative arts, nothing to do with William Morris's socialism. They can readily be shrugged off as mere surface to the text.[32]

It is 'moral realism' which deprives us (women) of our right to object to our (women's) place in 'socialist' utopia. That the women make tributes over the breakfast table – with bunches of red roses – may strike us, women readers, as funny and ironic in relation to how those roses figure in the current imaging of the Labour Party, but it will only strike the men as obvious, or an irrelevance. To labour the point via that image: the red rose has a strong iconography, as we all know, in the history of English poetry, but the meaning of that history for women (as red roses) is one that can be ignored precisely because it is so taken for granted, so encultured (encomposted).[33]

As long as the male Left cannot see what the literary does to the politics, they are not going to take seriously – see the serious point to – our tinkering with serving wenches. But remember, 'moral realism' is not in fact a piece of terminology coined in relation to *News From Nowhere* or *A Dream of John Ball*. 'Moral realism' is a coinage of Thompson's for a looked-for conjunction between 'experience' and Marxism – a conjunction he finds in the exemplary his-story of William Morris. But there is no such thing as *a* moral realist – William Morris. There is a realist text, replete with its moralism (the moral realist text) – a moralism which relies on *art* and on the *family* to carry its burden. And if we can't persuade the Left to take seriously what English socialist theory does for women's politics in *News From Nowhere*, we can have a try at disturbing them with what the 'moral realism' which recuperates Morris for Marxism does to Jane Morris: how in 'biography', where the family is more substantial than surface in the text, the moralizing of Morris aestheticizes *his* family, and erases all class critique of the social relations within it.

For a start, it is all-too easy to juxtapose the Jane Morris of Thompson's *William Morris* with Henry James's contemporary (self-consciously literary) Jane – indeed, Thompson himself juxtaposes them:

> Jane Burden was only seventeen when she was thrown (in the days of the Oxford Union) into the constant company of this group of artists in their deepest medieval phase. Her melancholy, large-eyed beauty struck all who knew her. Perhaps the young girl was swept into the role of Guenevere and Iseult before she herself had found out who she was. In 1869, ten years after her marriage to Morris, she seemed to Henry James the very type of 'Pre-Raphaelite womanhood':
>
> > Oh, *ma chère*, such a wife! *Je n'en reviens pas* – she haunts me still. A figure cut out of a missal – out of one of Rossetti's or Hunt's pictures: to say this gives but a faint idea of her, because when such an image puts on flesh and blood, it is an apparition of fearful and wonderful intensity. It's hard to say whether she's a grand synthesis of all the Pre-Raphaelite pictures ever made – or they a 'keen analysis' of her – whether

she's an original or a copy. In either case she is a wonder. Imagine a tall lean woman in a long dress of some dead purple stuff, guiltless of hoops (or of anything else, I should say), with a mass of crisp black hair heaped into great wavy projections on each side of her temples, a thin pale face, a pair of strange, sad, deep, dark Swinburnian eyes, with great thick black oblique brows, joined in the middle and tucking themselves away under her hair . . . a long neck, without any collar, and in lieu thereof some dozen strings of outlandish beads – in fine complete.

But of her character all accounts are reticent: she is silent, languorous, frequently unwell or supposedly unwell, occasionally high-spirited and good-humoured in more intimate company. Few accounts go beyond such appearances, and all dwell upon her remarkable melancholy beauty. The truth is more difficult to penetrate: but one thing at least seems to be clear. William Morris had married not her, but a picture, an ideal from his Pre-Raphaelite dream-world. The dream-world was so all-embracing in these years that it unfitted him for an equal human relationship. It was no fault of hers that, when the dream passed away and he came to know her as a real person, she was not suited to the fuller relationship he then desired. It certainly was no fault of hers: indeed, when this time came she was already so moulded to his dream that she could not change the poses and affectations he had helped to create.[34]

It is going to be hard indeed for biographer or reader to 'find out who [Jane Morris] was', when here (her third appearance only in the life-story) she is already twice over 'standing for' something other than her class and gender self.[35] In the James piece she is a Pre-Raphaelite picture. In the Thompson, the Pre-Raphaelite picture of the James piece is taken to *be* her, and William Morris has married it ('William Morris had married not her, but a picture, an ideal from his Pre-Raphaelite dream-world'). In other words, James's 'literary' picture of Jane Morris is taken by Thompson directly as 'evidence' to the historian's text: and as the means by which he gauges William Morris's progress towards 'moral realism' ('The dream-world was so all-embracing in these years that it unfitted him for an equal human relationship' – his 'ideal' is not the morally real, but that's no fault of *hers*). Thompson takes 'the picture' from James and assumes (as do all subsequent biographers) that it coincides with Jane Morris. From then on Jane Morris functions in two ways. Despite 'all accounts [being] reticent' as to 'her character', that initial production of her as an aesthetic – the picture – allows Thompson to describe her entirely within the domain of the 'literary', and thereby to demarcate the area of social relations in which Jane figures as exclusively that of *family* relations.[36] Wherever Jane *figures* (that is, wherever her presence in the narrative carries weight for the exploration of 'values' and 'ideals') Thompson 'sees' Pre-Raphaelite beauty: 'Rossetti discovered the beautiful Jane Burden, with her deep mystic eyes, shapely neck, and plenitude of dark hair, who was to become William Morris's wife.'[37] The tower-neck, pale ivory face, black crinkly hair, that 'certain massiveness' which make up for Thompson and all subsequent biographers the unproblematic compound called Jane Morris invariably prompts the biographer to reflect on William Morris's marital relations.[38] That is what seeing Jane Morris does to the account. From this juxtaposition of the woman's aesthetic and family, Thompson extracts the 'values' which are the justification for William Morris as Romantic *and* Revolutionary. This is how Thompson writes William Morris in history (writes him via the literary).

The original context of the James piece is a letter to his sister, Alice James. Henry James shares with his cultivated sister a joke about the Pre-Raphaelites. His sister shares his literary context, knows about Swinburne and Tennyson, shares his *artistic* reference, knows about Rossetti and Hunt. He jokes with her about walking into a drawing room and finding a Pre-Raphaelite picture. Is 'Jane Morris' an 'original' or a 'copy'? The terms of reference remain within that joke about art. In the original letter, James follows this passage with more reference to 'the whole scene':

> There was something very quaint and remote from actual life, it seemed to me, in the whole scene: Morris reading in his flowing antique numbers a legend of prodigies and terrors (the story of Bellerophon, it was), around us all the picturesque bric-a-brac of the apartment (every article of furniture literally a 'specimen' of something or other) and in the corner this dark silent medieval woman with her medieval toothache.[39]

The joke about the picture of Jane Morris extends to the drawing room, the family room, the family as a whole. In Thompson's account, a separation has to be made. William Morris has to be taken out of the picture. William Morris cannot be 'quaint and remote from actual life' because he is supposed to be a moral realist (but the picture makes him look ridiculous). Jane Morris can be left in the picture, since the family portrait is her *only place*, both morally and aesthetically.[40] The Thompson use of the James discredits it in that it fails to take the Jamesian tone of light mockery (not necessarily at Jane Morris's expense, but at that of the Pre-Raphaelite brotherhood). The James description is self-consciously literary ('She haunts me still' – as women in art do haunt literary men), but Thompson takes that literariness as a given. She *was* a picture. He starts from there (Jane Morris framed). He falters momentarily – 'the truth' about her 'melancholy beauty' is 'more difficult to penetrate', but that glimpse of untruth is not enough to interrupt the direction of his narrative. He proceeds to moralize her from this aesthetic premise – and in order to explain and later justify William Morris ('it was no fault of hers', 'it certainly was no fault of hers': but why maintain all this, if not to prove that in the end it's going to be her fault?).

It is not primarily the misuse of James that is at issue here, or at least, not at the level of the admissibility or otherwise of 'literary' evidence. The use of the James shows up again what we have been saying throughout this account, about what Thompson requires Raymond Williams to stand for in making good his version of William Morris.

Williams provides for Thompson the legitimation for what he found he had done in *William Morris* (a legitimation *after* the event), and felt the need to justify (in the 1976 'Postscript', which Anderson calls 'one of Thompson's most important political and theoretical statements in its own right').[41] As we said in Chapter 2, Thompson's early reservations about *Culture and Society* are to do with his commitment to history – and to a historical method which sees a raw material of 'experience' outside of culture. What the invoking of Williams allows Thompson to do is to 'handle' that experience via culture without having to explain his own cultured assumptions in doing so. That is what Raymond Williams covers for in Thompson. Question: why had Thompson chosen William Morris for that first book and for his particular purposes with it? Answer: because William Morris, artist and family man, is saturated in English bourgeois values, and that is what is going to make good Marx. Retrospectively Williams stands in for everything Thompson cannot face up to about this choice. How else could Thompson convince himself that William Morris represents a break from the nineteenth-century bourgeois liberalism in which he is so evidently at home? Shielded by Williams, Thompson cannot see that the supposed break from bourgeois liberalism – the break represented by 'the river of fire' – has carried too much of 'the bourgeois' with it – the aesthetic, the family – in the very process of narrating 'the river of fire': too much which blocks the narrator's view of nineteenth-century capitalism and its social relations. Thompson's Morris takes on the appearance of one of those oppositional voices which speak in *Culture and Society*, but the eventual claim for him, in the 1976 'Postscript', is for much more than that, for being uniquely situated in that.

As a historian and biographer, Thompson thinks he is writing about William Morris's *experience*, but he has adopted the mode of the Leavisite literary critic, resting on assumptions drawn from the ethics of aesthetics (and later he can turn to Williams to legitimate this as 'oppositional'). He narrates and critically explicates William Morris without ever recognizing that he is dealing in textuality.

We asked the question: Why had Thompson chosen William Morris for that first book and for his particular purposes with it? And we offered the *partial* answer: because William Morris, artist and family man, is saturated in English bourgeois values, and that is what is going to make good Marx. But the fact that the pre-industrial and medieval are integral to any account of Morris (whatever his politics) has a further attraction for Thompson. Morris's early aspirations for alternative social relations were articulated within the Pre-Raphaelite brotherhood in terms of archaizing poetry and the decorative arts. When, therefore, Thompson establishes the crucial terms of Morris's new kind of sensibility in the early chapters of *William Morris* he does so *in terms of* a set of medieval ideals which he maintains strikingly contrast with the ugliness and crudeness of bourgeois Victorian values. Thereafter, whenever Thompson wishes to distinguish Morrisism from Victorianism, he simply substitutes medievalism (an aesthetic and a set of values). Thus one of the attractions of the James passage (to return to it once more) is the ease with which it allows Thompson to produce Morris's moral realism not merely in terms of that family portrait, but a portrait in medieval costume, in which problems with post-industrial family relations can be glossed over. Anderson knows that medievalism represents a 'regression behind the range of potential occupations in capitalist society' which 'celebrates an essentially similar physical dexterity in homes, on the roads, or in the fields', yet even he is prepared to condone this as utopian.[42]

When Thompson comes on to Morris's socialism, the account carries over the pre-industrialism in ways which make it possible to ignore the class-specificity of nineteenth-century bourgeois social relations and the Victorian division of labour. Juliet Mitchell saw that, and furthermore she saw how that medieval family falsified the evidence and damaged the position of women:

> Industrialism *does* separate the family from its earlier immediate associations with the economy and this separation prevents in any case the total coincidence of the family and private property. It seems that Quintin Hoare is asking us to analyse the position of women in pre-industrial conditions. . . . 'What specifies the position of women in history *until the industrial revolution* ([Mitchell's] italics) is that her participation in production is mediated through the family'. To concentrate on this pre-industrial area – even assuming the hypothesis is correct – would be to write history with a vengeance.

This is the burden that Jane Morris carries in Thompson's account – her appearance stands in for Morris's 'oppositional' values and conveniently masks Victorian class relations (erases her class and compensates for his).

By the time that Thompson has arrived at the writing of *The Making of the English Working Class*, his interest in 'experience' has shifted to the grass roots, to the working class:

> I am seeking to rescue the poor stockinger, the Luddite cropper, the 'obsolete' hand-loom weaver, the 'utopian' artisan, and even the deluded follower of Joanna Southcott, from the enormous condescension of posterity. Their crafts and traditions may have been dying. Their hostility to the new industrialism may have been backward-looking. Their communitarian ideals may have been fantasies. Their insurrectionary conspiracies may have been foolhardy. But they lived through these times of acute social disturbance, and we did not. Their aspirations were valid in terms of their own experience; and, if they were casualties of history, they remain, condemned in their own lives, as casualties.[43]

The earlier book, *William Morris*, had supplied the method and approach: just as Williams's *Culture and Society* had supplied the approach (about which Thompson has reservations in that much-cited review) which was to characterize *The Long Revolution*. So the methodology of *William Morris* is made to give the illusion that in *The Making of the English Working Class* can be found the experience of both women and men in history. But the cultured narrative of *William Morris* has mutilated women's experience.

When Thompson wrote *William Morris* he was not ready to foreground working-class experience in radical history. He was not prepared to notice that Jane Burden was working-class, except in the beauty without brains stereotype. A graphic way of illustrating this is to juxtapose Thompson's account of how Jane Burden met William Morris with Jack Lindsay's:

> Jane Burden was only seventeen when she was thrown (in the days of the Oxford Union) into the constant company of this group of artists in their deepest medieval phase. Her melancholy, large-eyed beauty struck all who knew her. Perhaps the young girl was swept into the role of Guenevere and Iseult before she herself had found out who she was.[44]

> At some date in October Morris met Jane Burden. After the day's work, he, BJ, and Rossetti had gone to the Oxford theatre. They sat behind two girls, Jane and Elizabeth, daughters of Robert Burden of 65 Holywell Street. (Hughes also was there, says the BJ account, which puts Jane in a box above the artists.) In an effort to make the family respectable, Burden was later described as a livery stable-keeper; but someone who knew him told Mackail that Jane was 'daughter of one of Simmonds' men at the stables in Holywell'. Rossetti, who had long worked out the technique of picking up girls in the character of an artist admiring their charms, talked to the two Burden girls, attracted especially by the elder one, Jane. After some discussions Jane agreed to sit for him and his friends.[45]

In the second passage class is in play (and the morals of the brotherhood are also in play); but in Thompson Jane's beauty paints over her class and dignifies their behaviour. With hindsight what confronts us in Thompson's formation is the question: Why is Jane Morris a 'melancholy beauty' (promising to make an unsatisfactory wife), and not a working-class girl? (And the answer to that question should also answer why serving-wenches in *News From Nowhere* are red roses and not domestic drudges.)

He could scarcely have chosen anyone less suitable than a girl like Janey, with her own difficult set of problems. On the other hand he would have found it almost impossible to fall in love with a middle-class girl expecting the conventional responses and reactions. Janey had the virtue of being a working-class girl and yet seeming a remote medieval figure, who could have been a queen. So he could build his fantasy-life afresh around her, withdrawn from all middle-class calculations and constructing his own private island, garden, hall.[46]

This quote, from another Marxist historian, accidentally sheds some light on Thompson's position. The traditional Marxist knows that working-class origin is a 'virtue' for his history; the Morrisist Thompson 'build[s] his fantasy-life afresh around her, withdrawn from all middle-class calculations' (she could have been a queen). Beauty is now her virtue, and her class doesn't matter: for Thompson the 'virtue' of his Janey seems to *depend on* a negation of working-class consciousness:

Perhaps unresponsive by nature
   perhaps spoilt by the attention of poets and painters
   she had allowed herself to fall into a character of inaccessible beauty
   the airs of a Guenevere
   every approach (as it seemed to Morris) was met by Janey's passivity, her melancholy self-absorption
   on Janey's side he surmised not an unwillingness, but an inability to respond
   Janey, it seems, was not the kind of person to take much blame upon herself
   as she grew older, her personality seems to have grown less, rather than more, sympathetic, and her air of aloof discontent to have become more marked
   Jane Morris, in her spoiled and indifferent way, was hostile to Morris's Socialist views, activities and friends.[47]

We can only conclude that Jane Burden's 'virtue' was the absence of any experience which could be valued by radical history. What hope for working-class consciousness gendered female? The need for the male in this to be moralized via bourgeois art and the bourgeois family means that working-class experience can never be articulated except via those values: and because the female is functional to that model, her working-classness cannot appear at all (except as 'virtue').

When Thompson does come to focus on working-class experience in *The Making of the English Working Class*, he carries over 'moral realism' from *William Morris*. His declared goal of 'rescu[ing] the poor stockinger, the Luddite cropper, the "obsolete" hand-loom weaver, the "utopian" artisan, and even the deluded follower of Joanna Southcott, from the enormous condescension of posterity' – in other words, of making English working-class experience *respectable* – entitles him to use those techniques for endowing experience with 'value' which he had operated in *William Morris*. In the later book such a strategy is probably admissible (just as socialists have accepted the same strategies from Orwell on behalf of the twentieth-century poor). But what is admissible within the Thompson enterprise of retrieving working-class consciousness as a 'suitable' topic for historians is going to be a problem for subsequent radical history, particularly when social history belatedly remembers the women. The 'value' of working-class men's experience is authorized by culture, and in that account the women provide the 'virtue' via the family. But in that case the women will always appear in the account *as* bourgeois. Working-class woman in the family will either lose her class (like Janey) or lose her virtue (and we shall see in a later chapter that that is the difficulty with Hannah Cullwick); and in that case there is no account available to be given (within that so-called radical history) of women's class-consciousness.

Chapter Four

Talking her way out of it
From class history to case history

The problem of the subordination of women and the need for their liberation was recognised by all the great socialist thinkers of the nineteenth century. It is part of the classical heritage of the revolutionary movement. Yet today, in the West, the problem has become a subsidiary, if not an invisible element in the preoccupations of socialists. Perhaps no other major issue has been so forgotten. In England, the cultural heritage of Puritanism, always strong on the Left, contributed to a widespread diffusion of essentially conservative beliefs among many who would otherwise count themselves as 'progressive'. A *locus classicus* of these attitudes is Peter Townsend's remarkable statement: 'Traditionally Socialists have ignored the family or they have openly tried to weaken it – alleging nepotism and the restrictions placed upon individual fulfilment by family ties. Extreme attempts to create societies on a basis other than the family have failed dismally. It is significant that a Socialist usually addresses a colleague as 'brother' and a Communist uses the term 'comrade'. The chief means of fulfilment in life is to be a member of, and reproduce a family. There is nothing to be gained by concealing this truth.'

(Juliet Mitchell, 1966)[1]

In the article Lacan's theory is presented in terms which, despite all precautions, have 'culturalist' overtones (whereas Lacan's theory is profoundly *anti*-culturalist).

On the other hand, the suggestions at the end of the article are correct and deserve a much extended treatment, that is, the discussion of the forms of *familial ideology*, and the crucial role they play in initiating the functioning of the instance that Freud called 'the unconscious', but which should be rechristened as soon as a better term is found.

This mention of the forms of familial ideology (the ideology of paternity–maternity–conjugality–infancy and their interactions) is crucial, for it implies the following conclusion – that Lacan could not express, given his theoretical formation – that is, that *no theory of psychoanalysis can be produced without basing it on historical materialism* (on which the theory of the formations of familial ideology depends, in the last instance).

(Letter from Louis Althusser to *NLR* concerning his article 'Freud and Lacan', 1969)[2]

We return in this chapter to that second important debate in *New Left Review* in the 1960s 'which did not hit the Left headlines at the time (indeed, which was probably unfortunately masked by the noisier polemic), yet which was bound up significantly in the same debate, and came (as we shall show) to exert an equally strong influence', which we touched on in Chapter 2. While Perry Anderson and E. P. Thompson were locked in polemic (in the engine room), Juliet Mitchell was responding to Raymond Williams and Louis Althusser in her own way – a way which was to be just as influential, but which has never, so far as we know, been traced back to that crucial period of confrontation between 'history', 'culture', and 'Marxism'. To which Mitchell added 'feminism', and was promptly excommunicated by the *NLR* fraternity.

Mitchell's 'Women: *The Longest Revolution*', first published in *New Left Review* in 1966, sets out to put back women in socialist theory via a full account of women's social relations. The family is where she finds that women do enter the classic account (Marx and Engels), but where the simple *invoking* of the family as a stage in an argument ultimately focused on the male workplace *submerges* women, instead of including them. (At precisely that moment Thompson too is invoking the family, in the debate about that 'peculiarly English' Marxism, to provide the moral realism of his account.)

Juliet Mitchell wrote 'Women: *The Longest Revolution*' for her 'New Left Review friends and colleagues' and (as we point out in Chapter 2) the article acknowledges Raymond Willliams's *The Long Revolution*. That acknowledgement is made again (to remind the reader of an over-arching influence, perhaps) when the title of the article becomes the title of the book Mitchell published in 1984. But as we saw, the only acknowledgement of Juliet Mitchell's crucial contribution to Left debate in 1966 by those 'friends and colleagues' at *NLR* was Quintin Hoare's intemperate and disparaging rebuttal. On the link with Williams, Hoare and everyone else on the *NLR* board remained silent, and indeed Hoare's swipe at Mitchell may have pre-empted any serious attempt at considering such a link. Mitchell's interest in Althusser on ideology also occasioned neither response nor interest – when Thompson attacked Anderson and Nairn for their Althusserianism he ignored Mitchell's place in the debate, as did Anderson and Nairn in their responses.

Even though the male Left knew they should be dealing with 'the specificity of women', Mitchell's key assertion, in 'Women: *The Longest Revolution*', that in classic Marxism 'the family was never analysed structurally – in terms of its different functions'[3] was not seen as having any bearing on this. We have encountered this phenomenon once before. When Bea Campbell addressed working-class poverty, Gareth Stedman Jones (reviewing her *Wigan Pier Revisited* together with Williams's *Towards 2000*) could not see how her account had any bearing on the project he and Raymond Williams were agreed was vital – reconciling a feminist account with socialism:

> What Bea Campbell's book highlights is how much more difficult it will be to achieve a new form of alliance between socialism and feminism – let alone between men and women who aspire to be socialist and feminist – than is evoked by Raymond Williams.[4]

> One of the things now lacking within the feminist movement is male speech. Only when men, sensitive to a feminist case, begin to speak out their own difficulties more candidly, can there be a real chance of constructing the socialist and feminist vision of which Williams speaks.[5]

We said then that the desire for male speech was 'damaging to any attempt to narrate women in relation to the labour movement'.[6] Here we see that when Juliet Mitchell articulates the contradictions for women within classic Marxism's account of the family, Hoare says she misreads Marx. He cannot even hear her as engaging with the same political questions.[7] What he hears is something called 'traditional feminism': 'her position remains the traditional feminist one, which is in its essence moralistic'.[8] In *NLR*'s own terms (the terms of its long-running argument with the moralizing Thompson), this is to label her as 'bourgeois', and this is important.[9]

So the family was the stumbling block in the encounter between Mitchell's pioneering attempt at a socialist-feminist materialism and *NLR*. She formulated the issue in terms which they would not recognize, so that the contradictions she had indicated stood no chance of being resolved – they weren't even listening; they made the contradictions appear to be in her:

> This method is not a movement of the parts to the whole and back [no penetration, presumably] – not at any moment does she provide a totalizing synthesis, so that even in her conclusion the structures remain separate. The result is not only non-Marxist (that is, non-social, ahistorical), it is also sterile.[10]

In what follows it will be important to remember that there are *two* sets of problems here. There are the contradictions *within* the classic Marxist account of woman and the family, which it is Mitchell's overt aim to resolve. And there is the historical problem to which we have now frequently drawn attention – that the male account returns any such 'contradiction' unanswered to the female subject – it is Mitchell who is having the problems, not male Marxism.

Mitchell's interest in the family was a long-standing one, which had not until this point run into difficulties with her male Left 'friends and colleagues', but had been sustained in the separate strand of her work on literature. As she wrote in the preface to her collection of essays, *Women: The Longest Revolution*:

> I took my degree in English Literature and for ten years taught literature to university students. During this period – the 1960s – I was actively involved in politics, first in Marxist politics around the *New Left Review* and then in the feminism of the Women's Liberation Movement. I wrote both literary and political articles. At the time I thought of my work as going along separate but parallel lines. When I came to make this selection, I could see retrospectively their points of connection in myself. . . .
>
> In 1970 I gave up my university post. I wrote *Woman's Estate* (Penguin, 1972) and lectured freelance, mainly abroad, mainly on literature and the politics of feminism. The parallel lines started to come together and the underlying concern in literature and politics met in my growing interest in psychoanalysis.[11]

At this point we need to retrace our tracks to that earlier interest, which Mitchell draws attention to by the inclusion in her collected essays of two pieces on Emily Brontë's *Wuthering Heights* (a work which crops up repeatedly elsewhere in those essays): 'The focus, once more, is on my long-standing interest in the questions of femininity, in stories, and, once again – by now, for more than thirty years – *Wuthering Heights!*'[12]

The earlier piece was written in 1963 or 1964 – that is, at the same time as she was working on 'Women: *The Longest Revolution*'. The later piece was written in 1982, by which time she was a practising psychoanalyst. It is in these two pieces and in the more general debate on the Left about *Wuthering Heights* (it is curious how hotly the Left contested intellectual ownership of this piece of women's writing) that we can begin to see how easy it would be for Mitchell to be driven in the direction of the literary/psychoanalytical under the pressure of that refusal by *NLR* to acknowledge her work on the family as any kind of contribution to Marxist theory (consigning her account to the literary), and their insistence that it was her problem anyway (in need of the talking cure).

In her introduction to the first piece about *Wuthering Heights*, Juliet Mitchell comments that she had originally written the piece at a time when 'there was a movement away from Leavisite criticism and the beginning of an interest in using psychodynamic analyses of novels'. So that, like Williams, she sees Leavis as in some sense a starting point; and the attention she gives to Emily Brontë stands in contrast to (is oppositional to) a critical approach which relegates 'The Brontës' to a half-page note at the end of Chapter 1 of *The Great Tradition*, and in which Emily Brontë is dispatched as follows: 'The genius, of course, was Emily. I have said nothing about *Wuthering Heights* because that astonishing work seems to me a kind of sport [freak]. It may, all the same, very well have had some influence of an essentially undetectable kind.'[13] But she also claims that 'in a wider context there was the humanism of Raymond Williams, and the concerns of Richard Hoggart and Stuart Hall. Generously interpreted, psychological understanding of fictional characters fitted in there, too.' It is that 'generously interpreted' which interests us (her anxiety to invoke Williams again, as that 'longest revolution' of the book's title does also). There was a critical movement away from Leavis towards 'an interest in using psychodynamic analyses of novels', and there was a critical movement away from Leavis towards an oppositional version of culture and the access it gave to class-consciousness. Mitchell wants them to run in parallel ('generously interpreted', the one fits in with the other).

So it is instructive to look at the ways in which Mitchell's interest in *Wuthering Heights* is and is not Williamsite (is and is not Leavisite):

> Immune from the disintegrating effects of urban industrialism, Emily Brontë's romanticism is not the straining after golden-age pastoral ideals that makes and mars some of Dickens' tortured work; nor is it the bizarre, reintegrating construct of a genius like Blake. Like all Romantics, Emily does try to render whole what is splintered. But the disruptive agent is not for her, as it was for her contemporaries and successors, the industrial revolution; nor, as it was for her sisters, the discrepancy between personal experience and conventional morality. The divisive world that Emily tried to unite was more fundamental than this.[14]

> Emily Brontë's unusual existence: her isolation from industrialism and her immersion in a family from which she almost never departed, enabled her to have certain insights which were unavailable to many of her contemporaries who were more subject to the conventions of Victorian custom and the alienating experiences of an industrial society. Above all, she felt that there should be continuous growth from birth to adulthood, and when this was prevented the cleavage was seen by her as disastrous. The experiences of childhood were as profound as those of adulthood. Maturity and immaturity interact in childhood and adulthood.
> The greatness of *Wuthering Heights* lies in the *rationality* of its romanticism: the dialectic between the two constitutes the whole form and force of the novel.[15]

In Juliet Mitchell's account, Emily Brontë is 'immune from industrialism' by virtue of her position *vis-à-vis* the family. The family supposedly provides Brontë with a special 'wholeness' on account of this immunity. In the first place, the Brontë household constitutes the only society Emily Brontë inhabits, and therefore, in the Mitchell account, *is* Brontë's society. Emily Brontë has a peculiarly intense view of society ('intensity must make up for extensiveness'), because 'Emily Brontë's society was so small that she was able to grasp nearly everything about it'. And further, because Emily Brontë never married – and was thus 'uncluttered with diverse experience' – the Haworth household remains the unique family (and thus the unique society) available to her; 'no marriage splintered her childhood from her maturity'.

Such an account of the woman's immunity to the industrial via the family is in strict contrast to what draws Raymond Williams to *Wuthering Heights*:

> The power and intensity of *Wuthering Heights* need no additional emphasis. The recognition has been given. The control of *Wuthering Heights*, the equally remarkable control, is now quite generally acknowledged. . . . Some critics have turned the discussion, rightly turned it, from the ordinary terms of romance – or from the more extreme emphases of the mystical and the melodramatic – and located *Wuthering Heights* in a social history. And it is certainly true that the Brontës lived in a border country, on the empty moors near a new and disturbed industrial area. Charlotte used this experience directly in *Shirley*, though backdating its events to the Luddites. And it has been argued that this same disturbance – the new industrial dislocation, the birth of an outcast class, dark, unprecedented and exposed – is at the root of *Wuthering Heights*; even, as had been said, that Heathcliff is the proletariat. But social experience, just because it is social, does not have to appear in any way exclusively in these overt public forms. In its very quality as social reality it penetrates, is already at the roots of, relationships of every kind. We need not look only, in a transforming history, for direct or public historical event and response. When there is real dislocation it does not have to appear in a strike or in machine-breaking. It can appear as radically and as authentically in what is apparently, what is actually, personal or family experience.[16]

In order to recognize industrial social relations in *Wuthering Heights*, it is not necessary, for Williams, to make Heathcliff the proletarian hero and to inscribe *Wuthering Heights* in social history.[17] Unlike Mitchell he recognizes that the family is not exempt from industrialism; and industrial 'dislocation' can appear 'radically and authentically' in family experience as much as in 'a strike or in machine-breaking'. But as the last sentence of this passage shows, he once again 'uses up' the family as the making of the male 'personal': 'When there is real dislocation it does not have to appear in a strike or in machine-breaking. It can appear as radically and as authentically in what is apparently, what is actually, personal or family experience.' The juxtaposition is of the public form of 'dislocation' and the private; but the *subject* is the same subject (on the one hand in the industrial, on the other hand in the home) and the map is of *his* social relations.

So even when Mitchell tries to lean her literary criticism on Raymond Williams, she can be told that she is *wrong* to isolate the family from the industrial. If she puts women in the Marxist family, then 'the family is a form of private property',[18] and woman is object to the male subject; if she removes the family from the classical Marxist account, she fractures Williams's and Hoggart's 'humanism'. What she is trying to do is to distinguish her account of the 'radical', 'authentic', 'actual' personal experiences of women in the family from that supposedly non-gendered account in which it is the man's personal which is authenticated in terms of 'family experience'. Once again it looks as if it were her fault for taking up that position (for staying with the family at the cost of the theory) and, once again, the fault is with the existing critical account (which cannot accommodate her questions, let alone provide answers).

By 1982 when Juliet Mitchell turns her attention again to *Wuthering Heights*, it is no longer for its 'astringent rationalism' ('*Wuthering Heights*: romanticism and rationality'):

> The woman novelist must be an hysteric. Hysteria is the woman's simultaneous acceptance and refusal of the organisation of sexuality under patriarchal capitalism. It is simultaneously what a woman can do both to be feminine and to refuse femininity, within patriarchal discourse. And I think that is exactly what the novel is; I do not believe there is such a thing as female writing, a 'woman's voice'. There is the hysteric's voice which is the *woman's masculine language* (one has to speak 'masculinely' in a phallocentric world) talking about feminine experience. It's both simultaneously the woman novelist's refusal of the woman's world – she is, after all, a novelist – and her construction from within a masculine world of that woman's world. It touches on both. It touches, therefore, on the importance of bisexuality.[19]

And 'the story of Catherine and Heathcliff is a story of bisexuality, the story of the hysteric'.[20]

Mitchell has not changed her mind – she still wants to account for Emily Brontë in terms of the family, and she still wants that account to tell us about women: 'We have to know where women are, why women have to write the novel, the story of their own domesticity, the story of their own seclusion within the home and the possibilities and impossibilities provided by that.'[21] But the loss of confidence shows: what was once a complete social world is now '[women's] own seclusion'; their authenticity within the family has become 'their own domesticity'. Juliet Mitchell takes the blame, and it is women who now shoulder responsibility for the failure of both Marxism and literary criticism to provide a coherent account of their position. The family has become the Freudian family, and the issues have been internalized. What was once maturity has become pathology: Emily Brontë's novel is now therapeutic writing, and any tension over social relations within industrialism has disappeared: 'Freud locates the process of treatment in the space and time of an inhabitual discourse, separate from ordinary life, and therapeutic for precisely that reason.'[22]

It is striking that at the end of the second essay, 'Femininity narrative and psychoanalysis', Mitchell can at least now question the position of 'women under bourgeois capitalism' – can at least now frame a question in apparently Marxist terms:

> I think the novel arose as the form in which women had to construct themselves as women within new social structures; the woman novelist is necessarily the hysteric wanting to repudiate the symbolic definition of sexual difference under patriarchal law, unable to do so because without madness we are all unable to do so. . . . If we are today again talking about a type of literary criticism, about a type of text where the subject is not formed under a symbolic law, but within what is seen as a heterogeneous area of the subject-in-process, I would like to end with asking a question: *in the process of becoming what?* I do not think that we can live as human subjects without in some sense taking on a history; for us, it is mainly the history of being men or women under bourgeois capitalism. In deconstructing that history, we can only construct other histories. What are we in the process of becoming?[23]

But the key statement of commitment here is a giveaway: 'I do not think that we can live as human subjects without in some sense taking on *a* history' (our emphasis). '*A* history' is not 'history' in Thompson's or Williams's sense, and Juliet Mitchell knows that. *That* history relegated women to the family in the sense in which we discussed it in the last chapter – 'used up' women in the act of providing 'moral realism' for the men. Her history is 'mainly the history of *being* men or women under bourgeois capitalism'; a 'history of being', the case history of the individual, the only place (in Juliet Mitchell's experience) where any history of women or for women is to be found. 'I do not think we can live . . . without . . . taking on a history' – taking it on herself, taking the blame for the silence, talking her way out of it, offering herself for therapy.[24]

The shift from ideology to psychoanalysis in Juliet Mitchell's thinking between 1966 and 1982 – of which those two essays on *Wuthering Heights* are symptomatic – which is also a shift for her professionally from literary critic to psychoanalyst, is anticipated at the end of her 1971 book, *Woman's Estate*. Chapters 8 and 9 are entitled, respectively, 'The ideology of the family' and 'Psychoanalysis and the family'. It is in Chapter 9 that Mitchell clearly begins to feel more comfortable with the whole issue of the family, which in Chapter 8 had, for her purposes (explaining the position of women under capitalism via the family), been fraught with 'contradiction' and 'paradox' – contradictions and paradoxes which are endemic to the classic Marxist *account* of ideology as it fails to deal with women precisely by relegating them to a 'family'. Whereas that 'and' of 'Psychoanalysis and the family' already tells us (what we already know), that the domain of psychoanalysis *is* the familial, with woman's special need for therapy a consequence of her having already been relegated there. In the transition from the one to the other we may readily detect that acknowledged influence of Althusser:

> It was Althusser's emphasis on the importance of ideology that I found most useful. His definition of it as 'the way we live ourselves in the world' seemed to me an insistent dimension in any analysis of women. It was one strand that led me forward to my subsequent interest in psychoanalysis.[25]

Althusser 'led [Mitchell] forward' to psychoanalysis by taking her back to Freud – in fact to Freud and Lacan, but at this stage it was to Freud that Mitchell (re)turned. In a crucial article, 'Freud and Lacan', which first appeared in English (translated by Ben Brewster) in *New Left Review* in 1969, Althusser 'authorised' a Marxist accommodation of Freud, and in particular of Lacan, as an invaluable part of an exploration of 'familial ideology' (or, as we would prefer, the family in ideology):

The suggestions at the end of the article ['Freud and Lacan'] are correct and deserve a much extended treatment, that is, the discussion of the forms of *familial ideology*, and the crucial role they play in initiating the functioning of the instance that Freud called 'the unconscious', but which should be rechristened as soon as a better term is found.

This mention of the forms of familial ideology (the ideology of paternity–maternity–conjugality–infancy and their interactions) is crucial, for it implies the following conclusion – that Lacan could not express, given his theoretical formation – that is, that *no theory of psychoanalysis can be produced without basing it on historical materialism* (on which the theory of the formations of familial ideology depends, in the last instance).[26]

At the very moment when the *NLR* editorial board was insisting both that Juliet Mitchell *must* situate her discussion of women in the family (where, according to Hoare, they inevitably are), and that a classic Marxist account had *no room for* discussion of the family at all, this last paragraph of Althusser's appeared to offer Mitchell an alternative. Not Lacan himself for 'familial ideology', because 'his theoretical formation' was crucially anti-materialist. But Freud's recognition that forms of familial ideology play a crucial role in the formation of the unconscious, coupled with Lacan's recognition that this formation is symbolic (and therefore in *culture*), and a Marxist commitment to the view that '*no theory of psychoanalysis can be produced without basing it on historical materialism* (on which the theory of the formations of familial ideology depends, in the last instance)'. Crucial also for Mitchell is Althusser's admission that 'in [his] article ['Freud and Lacan'] Lacan's theory is presented in terms which, despite all precautions, have "culturalist" overtones (whereas Lacan's theory is profoundly *anti*-culturalist)'. It is Lacan Althusser wants, because Lacan's is a *theory* of the unconscious, whereas Freud's was a clinical practice, a methodology, eschewing system in favour of accumulated case history and precedent law. But in the first instance it was to Freud that Mitchell turned, for a version of the unconscious which made it a site of ideology peculiarly appropriate to the woman's case – the case silenced by male Marxism, and even male Althusserianism.

It was not in fact until 1977, when she began to collaborate with Jacqueline Rose, that Mitchell made the transition from Freudian psychoanalysis (where that first eviction from *NLR* had sent her for therapy) to Lacanian psychoanalytic theory, and not until then that she herself lost ideology as crucial for the conjunction of a Marxist-feminist impetus with an interest in the unconscious. And even then, she retained her conviction that her by now total commitment to the unconscious as the place to talk about women was a commitment sanctioned as materialist by Althusser. When Mitchell reprinted her introductory essay from her collaborative work with Rose, *Feminine Sexuality: Jacques Lacan and the école freudienne*, in 1984, she called it 'Freud and Lacan: psychoanalytic theories of sexual difference', again (as with 'Williams and The Longest Revolution') alluding directly to the influence of Althusser never named in the text. And she prefaced it as follows:

> In very different idiom and speaking to very different questions, the interest in Lacan in this essay has some echoes of my interest in Althusser in 'Women: The Longest Revolution'. There women were nothing other than the different social and economic structures in which they were created; there was no essential category: 'women'. Lacan's work sets up that realisation at the very heart of the question of the construction of femininity.[27]

But Mitchell's watershed work for feminism on psychoanalysis had been published earlier, in 1974. *Psychoanalysis and Feminism* was an extended account of Freudian psychoanalysis, whose avowed aim was to make the methodology of psychoanalysis available to feminism (and to counter that version of Freud which 'the greater part of the feminist movement has identified . . . as the enemy'). This is the key work for seeing explicitly what it was Mitchell was trying to do. In it we can see that struggle to keep ideology (the ideology of Althusser and of 'the ideology of the family'), alongside a growing commitment to 'the unconscious' as the place where the lived experience of women is to be found and articulated (*within* the family of 'Psychoanalysis and the family'):

> It is because it appears as the ultimate rationality, that critics mistake the Oedipus complex for the nuclear family itself. On the contrary, it is the contradiction between the internalized law of patriarchal human order described by Freud as the Oedipus complex, and its embodiment in the nuclear family, that is significant.
>
> The patriarchal law speaks to and through each person in his

unconscious [*sic*]; the reproduction of the ideology of human society is thus assured in the acquisition of the law by each individual. The unconscious that Freud analysed could thus be described as the domain of the reproduction of culture or ideology.[28]

The unconscious is where Mitchell wants to go, on behalf of women, but she wants to take ideology with her. In our terms, what she is looking for is an alternative *account*, which will position women so as to make possible a discussion of women's class-consciousness – the discussion which we showed in Chapter 3 as being blocked off for her by *NLR*, as they followed in the steps of Williams and Thompson. For Mitchell the flight to psychoanalysis is a last resort: 'A rejection of psychoanalysis and of Freud's works is fatal for feminism. . . . If we are interested in understanding and challenging the oppression of women, we cannot afford to neglect it.'[29]

We are insisting that because of the absolutely sound *motives* for Mitchell's move from Marxism and Left politics to psychoanalysis (whether Freudian or Lacanian), the fracture of feminist psychoanalytic theory *from* politics was not apparent until it was too late (if, indeed, it is apparent even now). Interviewed together in the feminist journal *m/f*, shortly after the publication of *Feminine Sexuality: Jacques Lacan and the école freudienne* (by which time, we are arguing, that fracture had been effected but not acknowledged), Mitchell and Rose were curiously out of synchronization as far as a feminist politics was concerned. Asked why they had chosen to edit Lacan's texts, Rose said:

> Your book Juliet, on *Psychoanalysis and Feminism* had just come out and there was a whole atmosphere which had in part at least been produced by that book, which could be called 'a return to Freud for women around questions of sexuality.' Now, insofar as that return to Freud on the question of sexuality had gone hand in hand, had been informed by Lacan's rereading of Freud, it made a lot of sense to go back, or rather go on, to look at exactly what it was Lacan himself had to say about women.[30]

What interests us particularly is that phrase of Rose's: 'a return to Freud for women around questions of sexuality'. Mitchell had not, so far as we can see, invoked 'questions of sexuality' in *Psychoanalysis and Feminism*. Her 'return to Freud' had, as we have stressed, centred on ideology, and the access which the unconscious might give to *consciousness* for women.[31] And if one consults *Psychoanalysis and Feminism* (via the index), 'sexuality' is always and invariably used by Mitchell as a clinical term – to designate female *neurosis* in the classic Freudian sense – not as a linguistic formation (the 'discourse of desire' which is Rose's concern). In a later article, 'Femininity and its discontents' (1983), Rose uses that formulation again:

> For while it is indeed correct that psychoanalysis was introduced into feminism [by Mitchell] as a theory which could rectify the inability of Marxism *to address questions of sexuality* [our emphasis], and that this move was complementary to the demand within certain areas of Marxism for increasing attention to the ideological determinants of our social being, it is also true that undue concentration on this aspect of the theory has served to cut off the concept of the unconscious, or at least to displace it from the centre of the debate.[32]

Mitchell went back to Freud in 1974 in search of something indeed which was 'complementary to the demand within certain areas of Marxism for increasing attention to the ideological determinants of our social being'. 'Questions of sexuality', however, suggests not a return to Freud, but Freud as your starting point, framed in terms of Lacan (for whom discourse separated from the material base *can* be the issue since 'Lacan's theory is profoundly *anti*-culturalist'): Freud asks questions concerning sexuality – asks questions which can only be answered with the trajectory of an answer couched in terms of the sexual. Mitchell (like Althusser) initially hopes to appropriate those questions and answers, so as to excavate the position of women (under and in 'analysis') via the family in ideology. Only when Lacan's symbolic substitutes for Freud's therapy (after the collaboration with Rose) does she come to believe that problems of familial ideology are to be solved solely with reference to the unconscious (whereas in 1974 'the unconscious that Freud analysed could . . . be described as the domain of the reproduction of culture or ideology'):

> [For Lacan] the analysand's unconscious reveals a fragmented subject of shifting and uncertain sexual identity. To be human is to be subjected to a law which decentres and divides: sexuality is

created in a division, the subject is split; *but an ideological world conceals this from the conscious subject who is supposed to feel whole and certain of a sexual identity* [our emphasis]. Psychoanalysis should aim at a destruction of this concealment and at a reconstruction of the subject's construction of all its splits. This may be an accurate theory, it is certainly a precarious project.[33]

So by this time she is looking at 'what Lacan has to say about women', but that is a back-tracking of a much more serious kind, since what the male theorist 'has to say about women' was what Mitchell originally set out to avoid – from that exchange with Hoare Mitchell had made it clear that male speech could not be helpful to her project. By contrast, *Rose* concludes her introductory section to *Feminine Sexuality* as follows:

In these texts Lacan gives an account of how the status of the phallus in human sexuality enjoins on the woman a definition in which she is simultaneously symptom and myth. As long as we continue to feel the effects of that definition we cannot afford to ignore this description of the fundamental imposture which sustains it.[34]

For Rose the project is to account (via the male speech of Lacan) for the way we as women 'feel the effects' of phallocentrism; for Mitchell the project had been to refuse the male account, to analyse and *alter* the condition of women. Throughout that *m/f* interview, we suggest, the gap between Mitchell's political feminism and Rose's deconstructive Lacanianism (true to Lacan, but unhelpful for Mitchell's enterprise) is clearly visible – an omen of things to come.

On the eve of the 1983 general election, we find a painful (but we would by now say predictable) testament to a particular kind of loss of direction, specific to psychoanalytic feminism, whose 'discourse' has become fractured from the material by that wholehearted endorsement of (editing the texts of) Lacan. *Feminist Review* – going to press four days before polling day – took it as a form of feminism which could be invoked at that crisis point, and mistook its 'questions of sexuality' (the drama) for a politics. The editorial to that issue urgently raises the question of a feminist engagement with national party politics:

We are going to press four days before the election. The

likelihood of a second Tory victory is devastating for feminists. Deeply committed as it is to patriarchal values, the Tory party is poised to demolish all the limited gains made by the women's movement in the last fifteen years. Under the guise of a new family policy which appeals to the deepseated conservatism of British society Margaret Thatcher's family policy group has come up with a package of ideas which, if effected, would result in reducing the limited autonomy women have gained, both in access to an independent income and minimal welfare rights. The policies have a distinctly conservative inflection, emphasizing the rights and responsibilities of individuals, family provision for social need, and child-rearing patterns that encourage individual effort. Some socialists have been tempted to counter Tory proposals with another set of 'socialist' family policies which equally foster a pro-family atmosphere but offer support to families in coping with poverty, sickness and dependence. To do this is to ignore the feminist and indeed the socialist critique of 'the family' as an ideology and an institution oppressive to women.[35]

Here we are, exactly as we were in 1966, when Juliet Mitchell saw a Left ideology of the family as a stumbling-block to progress for the women's movement. In this context the editorial struggles to incorporate a contribution from psychoanalytic feminism as political in this sense:

In 'Feminism [sic] and its discontents' Jacqueline Rose makes an important reassessment of whether there is a radical potential for feminism in Freudian psychoanalysis. By looking at the institutional conditions in which Freud began, at aspects of its history and at the place of psychoanalysis in British political culture she argues that overall the psychoanalytic project has to be understood as a radical one. In this context she reasserts its centrality for feminism, especially in its description of the unconscious and of the contested production of the female psyche.[36]

The editorial slip from 'Femininity and its discontents' (actually the title of Rose's article) to 'Feminism' is all too telling. 'Feminism and its discontents' might have to do with a 'radicalism' we on the political Left would recognize. 'Feminism and its discontents' might be about the demands of the women's movement for adequate child-care and opportunities for job-sharing. But in fact 'discontents' is specific to psychoanalysis (*Civilisation and its Discontents*): 'Freud considered that "discontent" (roughly the sublimation and repression of desires) was a condition of civilization.'[37] And the argument that 'the psychoanalytic project has to be understood as a radical one' is made in terms of 'British political culture', a curious phrase coined by Perry Anderson in his 1968 article 'Components of the national culture' (which Rose both cites and takes allusively as title for her introductory section 'Components of the culture'). Because Anderson identified psychoanalysis as excluded from British post-war intellectual debate, and never 'naturalized' as other imported theories had been, it becomes for this very reason for Rose the specialism in which woman – silenced by the male account within British political thought – is allowed to speak, to speak *politically* and to speak *radically*. Psychoanalysis and feminism are lined up historically, fortuitously, Rose says, because 'British political culture' excluded both (and as a version of Mitchell's taking up with Freud she is probably right).

'Femininity and its discontents' contains the suggestion that feminism should give less attention to 'ideology' and place the unconscious at 'the centre of the debate':

> It will have crucial effects, for instance, whether psychoanalysis is discussed as an addition or supplement to Marxism (in relation to which it is then found *wanting*), or whether emphasis is laid on the concept of the unconscious. For while it is indeed correct that psychoanalysis was introduced into feminism as a theory which could rectify the inability of Marxism to address questions of sexuality, and that this move was complementary to the demand within certain areas of Marxism for increasing attention to the ideological determinants of our social being, it is also true that undue concentration on this aspect of the theory has served to cut off the concept of the unconscious, or at least to displace it from the centre of the debate. (This is graphically illustrated in Michele Barrett's book *Women's Oppression Today*, in which the main discussion of psychoanalysis revolves around the concept of ideology, and that of the unconscious is left to a note appended at the end of the chapter.)[38]

The whether/or construction here sets the psychoanalysis of *Psychoanalysis and Feminism* on one side, and the 'concept of the unconscious' on the other, and this is a formulation to which feminists return, with increasing emphasis given to the unconscious. Indeed, that parenthetical comment on Michele Barrett's neglect of the unconscious is one that continues to resonate, both in the general argument of ideology versus the unconscious, and *ad feminam* in relation to Barrett's key contributions to feminist debate. In *Women's Oppression Today* (1980) Barrett did indeed make the discussion of psychoanalysis revolve around the concept of ideology; she saw quite clearly that that was the grounds for Mitchell's 'appropriation' of it:

> Attempts to break away from reductionism, and to locate sexuality and gender identity in the specificity of historical ideological processes have culminated in the recent feminist appropriation of psychoanalysis. Juliet Mitchell's extremely influential work of recovery, *Psychoanalysis and Feminism* has generated an interest in the possibility of using the work of Freud, and subsequent writers in the psychoanalytic tradition (notably Jacques Lacan), to develop a materialist feminist theory of gender and sexuality.[39]

The 'unconscious' is not simply 'left to a note' (actually a four-page expository note on 'Freud's account of psychosexual development'), it is deliberately left out of Barrett's version of Mitchell's strategic use of psychoanalysis to provide an account of 'the *mental representation* of social reality',[40] because for Barrett woman's 'lived experience' of social contradiction *must* be part of consciousness.[41] By 1987, however, Barrett is reproaching *herself* (taking the blame) for that supposed 'neglect' of the unconscious. In an article in *Feminist Review* she accepts responsibility (in another 'note', an autobiographical afterword) for having privileged 'ideology', and now passes this responsibility back to Juliet Mitchell:

> This 'social' perspective has now decisively declined in favour of a version of psychoanalytic theory that sees emphasis on the operations of the unconscious as in some sense *in competition* with a social theory of ideology. Jacqueline Rose, in an article that clarifies this development in a particularly sharp way, believes that the concept of the unconscious was in danger of being lost in these earlier appropriations of psychoanalytic theory. . . . [She] goes on to suggest that my locating discussion of psychoanalysis, in *Women's Oppression Today*, under the heading of ideology 'graphically illustrated' this general displacement of the concept of the unconscious. Whilst this may be true, it seems more relevant to point to the emphasis that Mitchell laid on the theory of ideology as the framework of her 1974 argument, and the extent to which this has now been rejected by a psychoanalytic sexual difference position.[42]

Barrett takes the blame, but at the same time cannot help mentioning that what she gave in *Women's Oppression Today* was an accurate account of Mitchell's position then, and one which (as long as they kept silent on the unconscious) she and Mitchell largely shared. By 1987 Barrett knows that Mitchell has rejected ideology for Rose and the unconscious, even if she cannot bear to make that explicit ('the extent to which this has now been rejected by [Mitchell and] a psychoanalytic sexual difference position'). This we feel may account for the confessional mode, and a further note at the end of the article which reveals that the pressure of the 'psychoanalytic sexual difference position' has caused her 'enough anxiety about an earlier version of this paper to cause me to rewrite it completely'. Taking the blame twice over, she rewrites the paper as atonement, as a recantation of her and Mitchell's earlier position ('for this protection from myself I am very grateful').[43]

But to drop 'ideology' from psychoanalysis is to put women firmly back in the family: not now the 'family in ideology' of the Marxist account, but the Freudian family as the place of confinement for women. Juliet Mitchell, in that 1974 argument, had continued to struggle with contradictions within the family and the problems that they pose for women (and she saw Freudian analysis as *exposing* those problems as lived experience – the female personal). By 1987, Barrett is apparently overwhelmed by psychoanalytic feminism's insistence on a 'politics' of the unconscious. The Rose article which she responds to, and which she repeatedly cites as *clarifying* the relationship between Lacanian psychoanalysis and feminist politics, closes as follows (on the eve of the 1983 election, remember):

> Psychoanalysis finally remains one of the few places in our culture where our experience of femininity can be spoken as a problem that is something other than the problem which the protests of women are posing for an increasingly conservative political world. I would argue that this is one of the reasons why it has not been released into the public domain. The fact that psychoanalysis cannot be assimilated directly into a political programme as such does not mean, therefore, that it should be discarded, and thrown back into the outer reaches of a culture which has never yet been fully able to heed its voice.[44]

Psychoanalysis 'cannot be assimilated directly into a political programme as such', and even if it is a place where 'our experience of femininity can be spoken as a problem', it is so in a culture which 'has never yet been fully able to heed its voice' (let alone her voice, let alone in protest).

Puzzled as to what 'political' might mean in such a context, Barrett herself closes in agnosticism, as to how psychoanalysis might clarify 'difference' as a key term in the relationship between the social and the female personal crucial for feminist politics: 'For the moment, the ubiquitous use of "difference" for such a variety of meanings is confusing. Sexual difference, positional difference and experiential diversity are best identified separately.'[45]

History Workshop of the late 1970s and early 1980s was also busy with questions of the relationship between psychoanalysis and feminism, and the implications of psychoanalytic theory for feminist historical methodology. In an exchange between Sheila Rowbotham, Barbara Taylor, and Sally Alexander over the term 'patriarchy', Sheila Rowbotham argues that 'it is not sexual difference which is the problem, but the social inequalities of gender':

> If we could develop an historical concept of sex-gender relationships, this would encompass changing patterns of male control and its congruence or incongruence with various aspects of women's power. It would enable us to delineate the specific shapes of sex-gender relationships within different social relationships, without submerging the experiences of women in those of men, or vice versa. If we stopped viewing capitalism and patriarchy as two separate interlocking systems, and looked instead at how sex-gender as well as class and race relations have developed historically, we could avoid a simple category 'woman'. . . . We could begin to see women and men born into relationships within families which are not of their making. We could see how their ideas of themselves and other people, their work, habits and sexuality, their participation in organisation, their responses to authority, religion and the state, and the expression of their creativity in art and culture – how all these things are affected by relations in the family as well as by class and race. But sex-gender relations are clearly not confined to the family (we are not just sex-beings in the family and class-beings in the community, the state and at work): like class relations, they permeate all aspects of life.[46]

'Sex-gender relations are clearly not confined to the family . . . they permeate all aspects of life', but Rowbotham's very insistence upon this acknowledges the fact that traditional Marxist history fails to carry over social relations in the family into 'the community, the state and . . . work' – there is a blank in the account where a politicized version of women's lived experience ought to be (and it is the theory which is at fault in this, not the evidence). Alexander and Taylor are equally preoccupied with that gap, but their response is to reaffirm that 'sexual difference *is* the problem':[47]

One of the most important breakthroughs in feminist theory occurred when women began to question this [biological] commonsense definition of sex, pushing past all the old assumptions about 'natural' womanhood and manhood to examine how deep the roots of women's oppression really lay. What was needed then, was a theory of gender itself, a new way of thinking about reproduction and sexuality. The search drew some of us towards structural anthropology and psychoanalysis. From a feminist reading of anthropology we learned that the social meaning of maleness and femaleness is constructed through kinship rules which prescribe patterns of sexual dominance and subordination. *From psycho-analysis we learned how these kinship rules become inscribed on the unconscious psyche of the female child* [our emphasis].[48]

Unlike Rowbotham, Alexander and Taylor perceive the blank as a silencing in history – there is no evidence of women's lived experience in a form available to the historian, even if she *is* a feminist historian. Their strategy on behalf of a specifically feminist history is to shift methodological ground to that of psychoanalysis, whose methodology is to detect (and provide therapy for) contradictions in the social in the disturbed testimony of the individual subject (most particularly, in the voice of the female hysteric). For them, women's experience is crucially lived *as* a problem, and is to be investigated where the problem is notionally located – in the unconscious. And although they invoke Mitchell's *Psychoanalysis and Feminism* in support of this position, there is a strong sense in which the whole problem seems to have become internalized with female subjectivity. Rowbotham's expanded 'history', which sets out to reinstate familial ideology alongside ideology in the work-place, and to confront the contradictions for women, is replaced by the individual woman's 'personal history', indeed her 'case history', as the only place where woman in history is authentically to be found:

> As feminist historians [write Alexander and Taylor] we share
> Sheila [Rowbotham]'s desire for more research into women's lives
> and experience. But this is no substitute for a theory of women's
> oppression. History only answers questions which are put to it:
> without a framework for these questions we shall founder in a
> welter of dissociated and contradictory 'facts'. Nor can women's
> own testimony about their relations with men be taken as
> unproblematic.[49]

On this account, woman in history is made to take responsibility
herself for those 'contradictions' between family and workplace. The
contradictions are internalized (she lives them), her testimony is not
unproblematic (it must be analysed and given therapy).

We have seen before how the temptation to make this move from
'class history' (where woman is silenced) to 'case history' (where at
least she speaks) came about, and this is the moment to remind
ourselves. In Chapter 3 we argued that E. P. Thompson's version
of radical class history depends on a 'moral realism' which takes the
bourgeois family from nineteenth-century ideology and literature, as
the touchstone for its 'values':

> Historical and cultural materialism cannot explain 'morality' away
> as class interests in fancy dress. . . . A materialist examination of
> values must situate itself, not by idealist propositions, but in the
> face of culture's material abode: the people's way of life, and,
> above all, their productive and familial relations.[50]

This moral realism produces the woman as bourgeois, in the family,
to give value to the male subject, whatever his class. As we said in
Chapter 3:

> 'Moral realism' is a coinage of Thompson's for a looked-for
> conjunction between 'experience' and Marxism – a conjunction he
> finds in the exemplary his-story of William Morris. But there is
> no such thing as *a* moral realist – William Morris. There is a
> realist text, replete with its moralism (the moral realist text) – a
> moralism which relies on *art* and on the *family* to carry its
> burden. . . . When Thompson [comes] to focus on working-class
> experience in *The Making of the English Working Class*, he carries
> over 'moral realism' from *William Morris*. . . . The 'value' of
> working-class men's experience is authorized by culture, and in
> that account the women provide the 'virtue' via the family.[51]

Under these circumstances, feminist historians in *History Workshop* (heavy with the weight of Thompson's methodological presence)[52] were almost bound to find themselves puzzled by the failure of the existing methodology to make room for a working-class conscious- ness gendered female, and to look (given their politics) to Mitchell for a methodological solution. And as we have now so often seen happening, the problem is doubled (compounded) by the fact that much of their work focused on nineteenth-century industrial develop- ment – the very period in which the *art* which provided Thompson with his 'moral realism' (and woman's place in it) was produced. So that feminist historians found working-class men in the communities they studied making *the very same moves* to give value to their bids for better working conditions and higher wages, and to claim support for their political movements.[53] In an influential article in *History Workshop Journal* (1983) Sally Alexander writes:

> I . . . want to point to the absence of the individual sexually differentiated subject in marxism. The question mark hovers over social being, and how it is experienced – by women and by men.
> 'Experience' of class, even if shared and fully recognized, does not, as Edward Thompson and others have suggested, produce a shared and even consciousness. Class is not only a diverse . . . and divisive . . . 'experience', but that experience itself is given different meaning. For marxists, meaning is produced through ideologies. . . .
> Debates within marxism which attempt to release ideology from its economic/material base are inexhaustible. . . . But if we step aside from these debates to ask not how are ideologies produced, but how, in Juliet Mitchell's phrase, do 'we live as ideas', then we enter the realm of social being and experience along another path – the path of subjectivity and sexual identity.[54]

She goes on to discuss the way in which for male workers in the 1830s and 1840s

> their status as fathers and heads of families was indelibly associated with their independence through 'honourable' labour and property in skill, which identification with a trade gave them. It was as fathers and heads of household that the radical artisan spoke of the loss of parental control and authority over kin, the predatory sexual freedom of the mills, the destruction of 'habits and morals'.[55]

As a result, although 'chartism was a mass movement of women as well as men which united all those movements against "bad laws and unjust legislators"',[56] the women (for instance in the declaration of the Female Political Union of Newcastle upon Tyne of 1843) expressed their grievances in terms of the interests of their '"fathers, husbands and brothers", and their place was in the home, from which they had been torn by poverty and the "scorn of the rich"'.[57] In the present context, we have encountered this effect before. Here, in spite of women's active participation in the movement, it is the Chartists themselves who 'moralize' their claim on behalf of 'honourable' male workers, by producing their women as distressed gentlewomen.[58] The public political speech of Chartism presents 'how the men feel' in terms of the (single wage-earner, bourgeois) family, in which the woman figures as 'virtue'. 'How the women feel' cannot be represented except in the identical terms: how the men feel about the women being deprived of that virtuous role in the family (but in fact those women are in the work-place).[59]

Alexander proposes solving this historical problem in locating 'how women feel' in the public speech of chartism by 'speaking of the [female] self and sexual difference', and she insists on the disruptive possibilities of such an approach (a strategy for the silencing of women by the historian, as well as a methodology for recovering 'a more generous conception of human consciousness'):

> In speaking the self and sexual difference feminism is at its most disturbing. Sexuality, intimacy, divergent conceptions of need are evoked and haunt the marxist historian with the spectre of bourgeois individualism, gossip, and the crumbling of working class unity. Ten years of women's history has calmed immediate fears. Few labour historians now hesitate to write of women's work, to mention the family or notice the absence of women from some forms of political life. Working class 'experience' has been stretched. . . . But if we are to pursue the history of women's experience and of feminism there can be no retreat from a closer enquiry into subjectivity and sexual identity.[60]

Comfortable with Thompsonian moral realism, the male radical historian hears the gendered language of the male worker, with its insistence on his headship of a household, his right to a 'family wage' for his 'wife and children', his right to be given dignity by means of a 'virtuous woman' at home, as 'history', as evidence of his 'humanity'.[61] Since it is *her* problem alone, apparently, the feminist historian appeals to the area where, according to the theory, women speak their inevitably fragmented and stifled self (fragmented and stifled by nineteenth-century patriarchal discourse, and by the labour historian) – the supposed articulation of 'feminine discontent'.[62] She does so on behalf both of her sisters in history and her sister historians:

> If feminism has been only one of the detonators of 'crisis' in marxist thought and practice it has been the most insistently subversive because it will not give up its wish to speak in the name of women; of women's experience, subjectivity and sexuality. . . . We were asking the impossible perhaps. As a feminist I was (and still am) under the spell of those wishes, while as a historian writing and thinking in the shadow of a labour history which silences them. How can women speak and think creatively within marxism when they can neither enter the narrative flow as fully as they wish, nor imagine that there might be other subjectivities present in history than those of class (for to imagine that is to transgress the laws of historical materialism)?[63]

Chapter Five

'Who speaks for history?'
The Left historian and his authentic subject

The autobiographical mode, widely espoused by the local history projects, is the mode of the long revolution, slower, acknowledging difficulty, mixing occasional insights into the prime causes and determinants of life – homelessness, redundancy – with experiences of sudden bereavement, a loving relationship, mental breakdown in the family, the party that lasted for three days, the failed attempt to emigrate. And who is to say that the latter experiences do not help us to clarify the complexity of the revolution we have ahead of us? . . . The problem is not the long revolution or the short revolution; history probably expects both. But which is best fought first, given the political formlessness and difficulties of our times?[1]

I am seeking to rescue the poor stockinger, the Luddite cropper, the 'obsolete' hand-loom weaver, the 'utopian' artisan, and even the deluded follower of Joanna Southcott, from the enormous condescension of posterity. Their crafts and traditions may have been dying. Their hostility to the new industrialism may have been backward-looking. Their communitarian ideals may have been fantasies. Their insurrectionary conspiracies may have been foolhardy. But they lived through these times of acute social disturbance, and we did not. Their aspirations were valid in terms of their own experience; and, if they were casualties of history, they remain, condemned in their own lives, as casualties.[2]

As a genre autobiography occupies an interesting position in relation to the expression or articulation of the subject. Within the parameters of the subject disciplines, it is not quite fantasy or fiction (in English), neither is it quite evidence (in History). It is this 'not quite' status which can frequently be seen in autobiographers' self-justifications drawn from conventions of naturalism in English and History: this is 'the true story', this is the tale of a 'real life'.

In History, in the late 1970s, the 'I' of autobiography attracted an entire debate about 'who speaks for history?', about the subjects and objects of History: a debate which tended to be framed in some problematic language about the relationship between the personal and the social. An exchange in *History Workshop Journal* sketches the map of that debate.[3] In 'Beyond autobiography', Jerry White argued that there are specific and important limitations to the auto-biographical mode. Autobiography, he wrote, lacks objectivity, is too parochial, and, most seriously, lacks a critical consciousness of capitalism. The autobiographical mode, in his language, 'distorts reality'. Stephen Yeo, in 'The politics of community publications', took up the position of antagonist in that exchange. He defended the autobiographical mode as that which 'history in general' needs. And then, in a move which, apparently without any sense of difficulty or awkwardness, conflates the 'autobiographical mode' with 'working-class autobiography', he argued that 'worker writing and community publishing has a lot to teach historians'. We, the historians, can learn from the workers.

Here, then, White, the historian, finds the autobiographers 'not quite' historians. They are not objective enough, and they are also parochial. If they are not historians, subjects – we assume from White – they must therefore be objects for the historian's use, evidence to form part of the historian's explanation. We, the historians, can use autobiography, if we are aware of its limitations. It can be *read* for History. It should not be *written* as History. Within this scenario of written and read, historian and evidence, subject and object, the human subject and author of the autobiography is thus conjured away and replaced by the subject historian, the subject History: and this sleight of hand – the historian's text displacing the autobiographer's – is performed in the name of 'the personal and the social'. The autobiographer in being 'personal', is found inadequate in the teeth of the bigger and better 'social'. White concludes by asking for 'a new synthesis' in which an intervention occurs: without consciousness-raising, people cannot understand the nature of their own oppressions. Autobiographers need conscious-ness-raising before they can become useful to historians. Auto-biographers (the people) return, in this way, to be told by us (the real historians) that they are subjects in need of consciousness-raising, or, rather, will be subjects after consciousness-raising: consciousness-raising, that is, by whom else, whom other than us, the real historians?

Yeo, by contrast, is at pains to allow autobiographers status as subjects, authors of history: they can be human beings who are also historians. But the matter of their being human beings is conflated with assumptions about class. Only working-class autobiographers – the real people from whom we can learn – are allowed to speak for the social via or in the personal. The argument is attractive in looking for authentic voices of a politicized kind, but it makes some strong assumptions about the relationship between consciousness and class. Working-class autobiographers can speak as subjects because they speak socialist consciousness. They speak socialist consciousness because they are working class. Socialist consciousness and a particular class position are, in this argument, the precise conditions for the production of 'authentic' autobiography. This time, the genre or mode of autobiography, the medium, the cultural form of the personal voice, is treated as transparent. And where, now, does Stephen Yeo, historian, stand, except outside this process, to the side of this cultural production, learning from the workers about socialist consciousness? By maintaining that he too can join in with the autobiographers (that no interpretation of text is involved), he writes himself in as ultimately *the* authentic subject, the historian, speaking the real subject, History: he, the author, creates the real text, albeit learning the language of that text from others – autobiographers – the little, 'not quite' historians.

More recently, there have been refinements and sophistications of these positions. David Vincent, in his study of working-class autobiography, suggests that autobiographies are 'units of literature'.[4] The Birmingham Popular Memory Group also emphasizes autobiography as mode or form with properties of genre which have to be dealt with: neither an expression of pure consciousness, nor vacant of historical consciousness until the latter has been raised. Yet again, though, 'the personal and the social' names the ritualistic diminishing of the autobiographers as subjects: 'Oral history and popular autobiography are forms which systematically individualize: yet an historically-informed political knowledge requires a much broader sense of social context.'[5] The delusion of both historical and textual approaches seems to derive from the pronounced 'I' of autobiography. In the end, for the historian it evokes a failure of objectivity, a lack of broad canvas, something personal which fails to incorporate or be something social.

The argument about autobiography reveals – or masks – an important argument about texts in History and texts as history. Autobiography, because of its emphatic 'I', which is a transparency, a vulnerability, becomes the historian's scapegoat for problems with 'material' and with other historians. Instead of History being the issue – the relationship between the personal and the social being a problem of all texts, all material, of History – autobiography becomes the issue, leaving our real historian free to patronize autobiographers, and perhaps more seriously, to maintain an unquestioned hierarchy of texts, of evidence, operating in the names of the lowly personal and the superior social. The problem is not that such a hierarchy might exist, but that it appears as given, naturalized, inevitable, and that, in appearing so, it perpetuates an unexamined place of authority and privilege for the historian who thinks himself real, as well as a good deal of confusion about the subjects and objects of history.

The commitment to the autobiographical mode which we introduce here came as the culmination of a struggle on the part of Left history to locate the voice of the working man *in* history. As E. J. Hobsbawm writes in the 1985 preface to his reissued *Labouring Men*:

> When [*Labouring Men*] was first published, the labour history which was most widely familiar was similar to conventional history: it dealt with the formal institutions – and the more or less straightforward political narrative of events and developments. The essays in *Labouring Men* were early exercises in widening the scope of labour studies in Britain, by looking at the working classes as such (as distinct from labour organizations and movements), and at the economic and technical conditions which allowed labour movements to be effective, or which prevented them from being effective. This wider form of labour history is now so well established that it is easy to forget how thinly this field was cultivated a generation ago.[6]

In this chapter we double back on ourselves, to take up that attempt by Left historians to look at 'the working classes as such'. Because we want to argue that, running alongside the intellectual currents which caused Juliet Mitchell to drift away from ideology towards the unconscious, there was another set within *history* pressing the male Left historian towards autobiography and individual agency. What we want to add to the argument of the last chapter (particularly as it was itself drawn, in its closing stages, towards debates in *History Workshop*) is that this parallel set of developments within social history apparently validated Mitchell's move – the two in some sense collided, over that term 'history' (and who speaks for it). 'Local history', 'personal history', 'case history', were all tending, we suggest, in the same direction, in a search for authenticity and agents in history, who had not previously spoken, or been spoken for.

We argued in Chapter 2 that in order to make the transition from *William Morris* to *The Making of the English Working Class*, E. P. Thompson needed a generalized way of talking about class which could carry the sense of the individual's ability to intervene in history, whatever his class position:

> What Thompson needs from Williams, and it becomes clear in the very critique he makes of Williams's *The Long Revolution*, is a particularly *literary* narrative, which can give agency to the characters of history, a narrative which is not the conventional one of the liberal historian, but one which can activate the categories of class and socialism.
>
> Raymond Williams's recovery of an 'alternative' tradition gives the illusion to the historian that he has discovered new agents in the making of history. And Thompson presents us with new agents (without ever feeling the need to theorise them), to support that explicit 'making' of English socialism, and above all the English working class, which is the lynch-pin of his version of history (but which was also the object of insistent theoretical attack from his opponents). It is the authentic experience of the newly-discovered agent, socialist man, which provides the momentum of his radical history.[7]

This is what we have described as the pressure of *moral realism* on the Left's historical narrative. In Chapter 3 we argued that by seizing upon this 'moral realism', indeed, by making it the distinguishing feature of his historical narrative, E. P. Thompson established a new kind of historical agency in the discipline, History. 'The appeal to the moral consciousness as a vital agency of social change' is the shaping conception behind Thompson's version of historical agency, and (as Perry Anderson recognized) it exercised an extraordinarily powerful effect on the emerging discipline of social history:[8]

> There is no doubt that the cadet group which remodelled [*New Left Review*] in 1964–1965 entirely failed to register the significance of Thompson's first major book [*William Morris*]. This can be seen most obviously in its denial of any important Marxist past in England – a wilful way of overlooking Morris, whose genius Thompson had declared to be 'peculiarly English'; but most essentially in its insensitivity to the major claim for Morris's greatness entered by Thompson – his 'moral realism': not only the 'practical moral example of his life' and the 'profound moral insight of his political and artistic writings', but 'the appeal to the moral consciousness as a vital agency of social change'. This claim is convincingly substantiated by Thompson's study.[9]

Our doubling back on ourselves here takes us back to a point just *before* Thompson's *William Morris* and his 'moral realism', to the developing concern on the Left with the particular problem of distinguishing between causal, retrospective accounts of the large movements in history – the Industrial Revolution, the rise of capitalism – and working-class *consciousness* of those movements, particularly the historical part played by the working classes in those developing movements. Did the working classes passively suffer the imposition of change? Were 'unsuccessful' movements aimed at altering the course of industrialization, such as the Luddites and the Chartists, failed attempts at historical agency, or had the historian's prior assumption of 'progress' erased or underrated a significant historical intervention? What does 'popular discontent' have to do with the contention that the 'standard of living' rose steadily in the nineteenth century under industrialization?[10]

E. J. Hobsbawm's 1952 essay, 'The machine breakers', typifies the Left historian's dilemma over how to explore and balance the relationship between large historical developments and working-class consciousness. The fundamental problem, according to Hobsbawm, is that post-industrial liberal ideology colours the account of working-class intervention in the industrialization process, and certainly prejudges the outcome:

> It is perhaps time to reconsider the problem of machine-wrecking in the early industrial history of Britain and other countries. . . .

In much of the discussion of machine-breaking one can still detect the assumption of nineteenth-century middle-class economic apologists, that the workers must be taught not to run their heads against economic truth, however unpalatable. . . . The conscious views of most students may be summed up as follows: the triumph of mechanization was inevitable. We can understand, and sympathize with the long rear-guard action which all but a minority of favoured workers fought against the new system; but we must accept its pointlessness and its inevitable defeat.[11]

The collective consciousness of the workers is tailored, on this account, to the historical outcome: 'thus, an excellent work, published in 1950, can still describe Luddism simply as a "pointless, frenzied, industrial *Jacquerie*"'. *Class* consciousness is subsumed under the rubric of the historian's own post-industrial consciousness. The issue, for Hobsbawm, is the retrieval of working-class consciousness in its historical context – reconstructing the strategic arguments and motives which produced a pattern of working-class intervention dubbed 'Luddism', as an effective means of countering coercion. Hobsbawm's own solution is to reconstruct a version of machine-breaking which respects the evidence, but which attributes political awareness and tactical astuteness to working men as a group, but one can readily feel the pressure for some continuous narrative of working-class response to events (of the kind Thompson would subsequently provide):

There are at least two types of machine-breaking, quite apart from the wrecking incidental to ordinary riots against high prices or other causes of discontent – for instance, some of the destruction in Lancashire in 1811, and Wiltshire in 1826. The first sort implies no special hostility to machines as such, but is, under certain conditions, the normal means of putting pressure on employers or putters-out. As has been justly noted, the Nottinghamshire, Leicestershire and Derbyshire Luddites 'were using attacks upon machinery, whether new or old, as a means of coercing their employers into granting them concessions with regard to wages and other matters'. This sort of wrecking was a traditional and established part of industrial conflict in the period of the domestic and manufacturing system, and the early stages of factory and mine. It was not directed only against machines, but also against raw material, finished goods, or even the private property of employers. . . . The second sort of wrecking . . . is generally regarded as the expression of working-class hostility to the new machines of the industrial revolution, especially labour-saving ones. There can, of course, be no doubt of the great feeling of opposition to new machines. . . . Yet three observations ought to be made. First, this hostility was neither so indiscriminate nor so specific as has often been assumed. Second, with local or sectional exceptions, it was surprisingly weak in practice. Lastly, it was by no means confined to workers, but was shared by the great mass of public opinion, including many manufacturers.[12]

'The machine breakers' first appeared in the founding issue of the historical journal *Past and Present* (of which Hobsbawm was assistant editor): *Past and Present* also was committed from the outset to the pursuit of an elusive working-class consciousness against the grain of contemporary historical accounts which tended to minimize the historical importance for change of the working classes (as opposed to the developing bourgeoisie). In the introduction to the first issue of that journal, John Morris and Hobsbawm wrote:

> Our main task, most of us would agree, is to record and explain [the] 'transformations that society undergoes by its very nature.' Such a study cannot but prompt some general conclusions, whether or not we call them 'laws of historical development' – though we shall be poor historians if we underrate their complexity. Men are active and conscious makers of history, not merely its passive victims and indices. Each form of human society, and each individual phase therein, has its own special laws of development.[13]

Here again is that emphasis on agency and consciousness as crucial for historical explanation: 'Men are active and conscious makers of history, not merely its passive victims and indices'. Here again, therefore, in the guiding principles of *Past and Present*, is the pressure towards an account of *class* consciousness which will entitle the Left historian, as part of his explanation, to attribute historical agency to groups other than the so-called 'governing' or 'ruling' elites.

As these debates focused on the nineteenth century, class- and labour-relations, and industrialization, as the preconditions for twentieth-century politics and society, 'culture' turned out to be the crucial component in a reconsidered historical explanation which took account of 'men as active and conscious makers of history'.

'Culture' defined the terms of debate; it was constructed as 'dominant', but those outside the dominant modes nevertheless had access to it; it bound community to consciousness in ways which were available for analysis. This vital explanatory role for 'culture' is set out with considerable clarity by Williams in the concluding chapter of *Culture and Society*, and recapitulated vigorously by Thompson, in what increasingly looks to us like the most importantly innovative and influential move as a Left historian, structuring the account in *The Making of the English Working Class*.

In *Culture and Society*, Williams had set up the distinction between bourgeois individualism and working-class consciousness in terms of the particular relationship of distinct groups of people with culture – where 'culture' is specified in the first place in the conventional literary sense as 'a body of intellectual and imaginative work':

> If we think of culture, as it is important to do, in terms of a body of intellectual and imaginative work, we can see that with the extension of education the distribution of this culture is becoming more even, and, at the same time, new work is being addressed to a public wider than a single class. Yet a culture is not only a body of intellectual and imaginative work; it is also and essentially a whole way of life. The basis of a distinction between bourgeois and working-class culture is only secondarily in the field of intellectual and imaginative work, and even here it is complicated, as we have seen, by the common elements resting on a common language. . . . The crucial distinguishing element in English life since the Industrial Revolution is not language, not dress, not leisure – for these indeed will tend to uniformity. The crucial distinction is between alternative ideas of the nature of social relationship.[14]

Here Williams insists that far from greater general access to culture (via a broader-based educational system, and improved communications) producing a more homogeneous society, the differing address of distinct class groups to that culture (their inequality *in* culture) means that culture itself provides the foundation for distinct class-consciousness.

'Bourgeois culture', although conceived of as individualistic, is nevertheless available as a source of non-individualistic group-consciousness – that specific consciousness which emerged in the early decades of the nineteenth century as working-class consciousness. Bourgeois culture is *available* to sustain such a working-class consciousness (according to Williams):

> 'Bourgeois' is a significant term because it marks that version of
> social relationship which we usually call individualism: that is to
> say, an idea of society as a neutral area within which each
> individual is free to pursue his own development and his own
> advantage as a natural right. . . . [T]he individualist idea can be
> sharply contrasted with the idea that we properly associate with
> the working class: an idea which, whether it is called communism,
> socialism, or cooperation, regards society neither as neutral nor as
> protective, but as the positive means for all kinds of development,
> including individual development. Development and advantage are
> not individually but commonly interpreted. The provision of the
> means of life will, alike in production and distribution, be collec-
> tive and mutual. Improvement is sought, not in the opportunity to
> escape from one's class, or to make a career, but in the general
> and controlled advance of all. The human fund is regarded as in
> all respects common, and freedom of access to it as a right
> constituted by one's humanity; yet such access, in whatever kind,
> is common or it is nothing. Not the individual, but the whole
> society, will move.[15]

These are precisely the terms in which Thompson defines class and
class-consciousness in the preface to *The Making of the English
Working Class*:

> Class happens when some men, as a result of common experiences
> (inherited or shared), feel and articulate the identity of their
> interests as between themselves, and as against other men whose
> interests are different from (and usually opposed to) theirs. The
> class experience is largely determined by the productive relations
> into which men are born – or enter involuntarily. Class-
> consciousness is the way in which these experiences are handled
> in cultural terms: embodied in traditions, value-systems, ideas and
> institutional forms.[16]

When Thompson comes to define the 'collectivist values' which
distinguish early nineteenth-century working-class organizations,
beginning with the friendly societies, he draws directly on this
account of Williams's of culture nourishing the working class's
'basic collective idea', as well as sustaining bourgeois individualism:

Mr Raymond Williams has suggested that 'the crucial distinguishing element in English life since the Industrial Revolution is . . . between alternative ideas of the nature of social relationship'. As contrasted with middle-class ideas of individualism or (at their best) of service, 'what is properly meant by "working-class culture" . . . is the basic collective idea, and the institutions, manners, habits of thought and intentions which proceed from this'.[17]

Thompson's own inclination is to interpolate 'lived experience' here, as stimulating the working-class commitment to communality. Nevertheless, the crucial collective values are consciously held (are established *as* working-class consciousness) via culture – and this is importantly Williams's point:

> Friendly societies did not 'proceed from' an idea: both the ideas and the institutions arose in response to certain common experiences. But the distinction is important. In the simple cellular structure of the friendly society, with its workaday ethos of mutual aid, we can see many features which were reproduced in more sophisticated and complex forms in trade unions, cooperatives, Hampden Clubs, Political Unions, and Chartist lodges. At the same time the societies can be seen as crystallizing an ethos of mutuality very much more widely diffused in the 'dense' and 'concrete' particulars of the personal relations of working people, at home and at work. . . . [By] the early years of the nineteenth century it is possible to say that collectivist values are dominant in many industrial communities; there is a definite moral code, with sanctions against the blackleg, the 'tools' of the employer or the unneighbourly, and with an intolerance towards the eccentric or individualist. Collectivist values are consciously held and are propagated in political theory, trade union ceremonial, moral rhetoric. It is, indeed, this collective self-consciousness, with its corresponding theory, institutions, discipline, and community values which distinguishes the nineteenth-century working class from the eighteenth-century mob.[18]

We suggested in Chapter 3 that there was a crucial relationship between E. P. Thompson's *The Making of the English Working Class* and Raymond Williams's *Culture and Society*. Here we see how from the standpoint of history this relationship centred on a shared understanding of the instrumentality of 'bourgeois' culture in the formation of (the *making* of) a distinctively working-class consciousness in England, in the early nineteenth-century. We shall want to argue, however (enlarging on themes we introduced in Chapters 2 and 3), that it is in the end *differences* between Williams's and Thompson's argument about the relation between class-consciousness and culture which confuse the Left debate about culture and class as it is conducted within History.

In Williams's account there is the assumption that it is culture which constitutes class-consciousness – which brings about a coherent perception by a non-dominant group of itself as a concomitant development. In Thompson's account, on the other hand, there is a consistent emphasis on the fact that experience precedes culture – that the group already allied in its labour relations and practices recognizes itself as a group via culture, that culture gives it its collective values. But what is strikingly common to both is the insistence that *class* as a focus for historical study 'entails the notion of historical relationship'. And they also share the belief that *as* a relationship class can be mapped, historically, on to (or at least in terms of) a period's intellectual and imaginative works – in other words, as a relationship to culture. We would want to stress here how highly idiosyncratic – how peculiarly English – this shared Thompson/Williams version of class is, and at the same time how tenaciously it has become embedded in the British Left's assumptions about consciousness:

> By class I understand a historical phenomenon, unifying a number of disparate and seemingly unconnected events, both in the raw material of experience and in consciousness. I emphasize that it is a *historical* phenomenon. I do not see class as a 'structure', nor even as a 'category', but as something which in fact happens (and can be shown to have happened) in human relationships.
> More than this, the notion of class entails the notion of historical relationship. Like any other relationship, it is a fluency which evades analysis if we attempt to stop it dead at any given moment and anatomize its structure. . . . If we stop history at a given point there are no classes but simply a multitude of individuals with a multitude of experiences. But if we watch these men over an adequate period of social change, we observe patterns in their relationships, their ideas, and their institutions. Class is defined by men as they live their own history, and, in the end, this is its only definition.[19]

Class connects individuals and their experiences; it is observable as 'patterns in their relationships, their ideas, and their institutions', in the ways, in other words, in which individuals relate their own experiences to available ways of rendering, and above all, *giving value to* experience in general, that is, to culture. All these formulations, it will be observed, characterize class in terms of consciousness – for the purposes of this kind of historical explanation, class *is* consciousness of a relationship with others, consciousness of an oppositional relationship with others (other classes). So 'class' and 'class-consciousness' become virtually interchangeable, and both are crucially connected with the ability of the (no longer privileged) individual to articulate his experience as *communal*:

> Class happens when some men, as a result of common experiences (inherited or shared) feel and articulate the identity of their interests as between themselves, and as against other men whose interests are different from (and usually opposed to) theirs. . . . Class-consciousness is the way in which these experiences are handled in cultural terms: embodied in traditions, value-systems, ideas and institutional terms.[20]

'Class happens when some men . . . feel and articulate'; 'class-consciousness is the way in which these experiences are handled in cultural terms'; 'class is defined by men as they live their own history, and, in the end, this is its only definition'. In a passage in 'The peculiarities of the English' which he himself cites in his 1968 'Postscript' to the revised edition of *The Making of the English Working Class*, Thompson recapitulates: 'When we speak of *a* class we are thinking of a very loosely defined body of people who share the same congeries of interests, social experiences, traditions and value-system, who have a *disposition* to *behave* as a class, to define themselves in their actions and in their consciousness in relation to other groups of people in class ways'.[21] 'Class itself is not a thing, it is a happening', Thompson writes, and he adds (as the concluding sentence of the 1968 'Postscript'): 'This book is an attempt to describe this happening, this process of self-discovery and of self-definition.'[22]

Set alongside the conventionally broad sweep of more traditional history, such formulations significantly disturb and disrupt the account. Social groups are not treated as objects or entities, but as assemblages of individual responses to, and testimonies to 'lived experience'. In traditional terms, 'when we consider measurable quantities, it seems clear that over the years 1790–1840 the national product was increasing more rapidly than the population';[23] in Thompson's terms, 'the "average" working man remained very close to subsistence level at a time when he was surrounded by the evidence of the increase of national wealth, much of it transparently the product of his own labour, and passing, by equally transparent means, into the hands of his employers. In psychological terms, this felt very much like a decline in standards.'[24]

The form Thompson's account takes is shaped self-consciously as a reaction *against* a type of historical explanation which reduces the experience of the working class to the outcome of a set of statistics and equations, and minimizes any sense of working-class intervention in historical process and change. In our present context (what constitutes the 'authentic' subject of history), it is worth considering what kind of historical explanation is yielded by a historical investigation which keeps the alternative objectives (working-class experience as intrinsic to the account, together with the 'felt' impact of altered economic conditions) consistently in mind. Certainly it is one which ascribes agency more widely, and more loosely. 'Dispositions' and 'behaviour' now figure in the account; 'self-discovery' and 'self-definition' have their part to play in the shaping of history. And if the nature of the final explanation is not entirely clear, some of its implications, by way of the challenge to orthodox accounts, are. In particular, if we return to the 'standard-of-living' debate, which concerned Hobsbawm because of the inadequate notion of 'improvement' it entailed (one which excluded the working man's own perception of his predicament as *worse* than prior to industrialization), Thompson's type of historical account manages to effect the desired problematizing intervention:

If we can now see more clearly many of the elements which made up the working-class communities of the early nineteenth century, a definitive answer to the 'standard-of-living' debate controversy must still evade us. For beneath the word 'standard' we must always find judgements of value as well as questions of fact. Values, we hope to have shown, are not 'imponderables' which the historian may safely dismiss with the reflection that, since they are not amenable to measurement, anyone's opinion is as good as anyone else's. They are, on the contrary, those questions of human satisfaction, and of the direction of social change, which the historian ought to ponder if history is to claim a position among the significant humanities.[25]

Definitive answers evade us, but we have retrieved a historically specific account weighted towards the response of the working class to the Industrial Revolution, which now becomes relevant to the historical explanation, in the form of the *cultural* version of events – the self-conscious, self-defining version. Instead of recording, tabulating and analysing the records of cost of living, average wage, the price of bread and meat, the historian

> is concerned with the values actually held by those who lived through the Industrial Revolution. The old and newer modes of production each supported distinct kinds of community with characteristic ways of life. Alternative conventions and notions of human satisfaction were in conflict with each other, and there is no shortage of evidence if we wish to study the ensuing tensions.[26]

He finds his evidence for the fact that the working man did indeed experience the Industrial Revolution as a *worsening* of his condition, an 'immiseration', in spite of material improvements in culture, in

> the 'romantic' critique of industrialisation which stems from one part of the experience, and by the record of tenacious resistance by which handloom weaver, artisan or village craftsman confronted this experience and held fast to an alternative culture. . . . Any evaluation of the quality of life must entail an assessment of the total life-experience, the manifold satisfactions and deprivations, cultural as well as material, of the people concerned. From such a standpoint, the older 'cataclysmic' view of the Industrial Revolution must still be accepted. During the years between 1780 and 1840 the people of Britain suffered an experience of immiseration, even if it is possible to show a small statistical improvement in material conditions.[27]

We are clearly shifting here in the direction of 'experience' as an intrinsic part of a historical explanation of change: how it *felt* to participate in the process is treated by Thompson as part of the data on which the generalized account must be based. And 'values' are doubly at issue here:

> For beneath the word 'standard' we must always find judgements

of value as well as questions of fact. . . . The historian, or the historical sociologist, must in fact be concerned with judgements of value in two forms. In the first instance, he is concerned with the values actually held by those who lived through the Industrial Revolution. . . . In the second instance, he is concerned with making some judgement of value upon the whole process entailed in the Industrial Revolution of which we ourselves are an end-product.[28]

The point is, the appeal to 'lived experience' takes us back again across the notional dividing line between historical and narrative accounts. At this stage in his argument (halfway through *The Making of the English Working Class*), Thompson once again reaches out towards Raymond Williams's 'oppositional' in culture, to bond 'experience' and 'values' on to working-class consciousness.

The commitment to values on the part of the historian reintroduces that 'moral realism' which we encountered in Thompson's work on William Morris, as importantly part of the construction of his biographical narrative.[29] This insistence that the historian must focus his account upon 'the values *actually* held by those who lived through the Industrial Revolution' (our emphasis), involves Thompson's invoking classic 'realism' in the same way we detected him doing in his *William Morris* ('"Realism", in the sense in which Thompson uses it . . . is part of that terminology which allows the critic to pass from art to experience – to produce art as that "totality" which builds values into a (specified) account of experience').[30] By maintaining that, in the process of framing such a historical explanation, the historian himself is 'concerned with making some judgement of value upon the whole process entailed in the Industrial Revolution of which we ourselves are an end-product' Thompson acknowledges that his is a *moral* realist account: by building into his historical account the values of 'perhaps a unique formation', 'this British working class of 1832',[31] Thompson claims to uncover a value-system of which we are ourselves the product ('*Moral* realism simply emphasizes that value-laden quality of the account').[32]

It should come as no surprise to us, therefore, to find that at this pivotal point in the development of his argument Thompson confidently introduces a passage from William Blake's *Prophetic Books* as historical evidence of 'experience' – 'the values *actually* held by those who lived through the Industrial Revolution':

It is neither poverty nor disease but work itself which casts the blackest shadow over the years of the Industrial Revolution. It is Blake, himself a craftsman by training, who gives us the experience:

> Then left the sons of Urizen the plow & harrow, the loom,
> The hammer & the chisel & the rule & compasses . . .
> And all the arts of life they chang'd into the arts of death.
> The hour glass contemn'd . . . & the water wheel . . .
> And in their stead intricate wheels invented, Wheel without wheel,
> To perplex youth in their outgoings & to bind to labours
> Of day & night the myriads of Eternity.[33]

In Blake's overtly moralizing formulation of the vicissitudes of the Industrial Revolution Thompson finds a historical 'voice' for non-elite experience, which is nevertheless composed in the recognizable evaluative terms of high culture.

The claim that Blake's romanticism gives access to such an oppositional social view comes directly from Williams. Blake's is an oppositional voice proposed by Williams in *Culture and Society* in just these terms – a 'record' of how the changes brought about by the Industrial Revolution were *felt* by those who dissociated themselves from the class-interests of the governing class:

> Of the . . . changes that we call the Industrial Revolution, the landmarks are less obvious; but the lifetime of Blake, 1757 to 1827, is, in general, the decisive period. The changes that we receive as record were experiences in these years, on the senses: hunger, suffering, conflict, dislocation; hope, energy, vision, dedication. The pattern of change was not background, as we may now be inclined to study it; it was, rather, the mould in which general experience was cast.
>
> It is possible to abstract a political commentary from the writings of these poets, but this is not particularly important. . . . In every case, . . . the political criticism is now less interesting than the wider social criticism: those first apprehensions of the essential significance of the Industrial Revolution, which all felt and none revoked.[34]

For Williams this is the moment at which 'culture' in his strong sense emerges; the moment at which art takes it upon itself to defend a 'mode of human experience and activity which the progress of society seemed increasingly to deny'.[35] Culture is a means of access to a version of experience which gives meaning to it, which provides the individual with consciousness of his experience, in his own class-group's shared terms. But for Thompson this is the *voice* of experience: 'It is Blake, himself a craftsman by training, who gives us the experience.'

For Thompson, Blake's *Prophetic Books* are a record of the craftsman's experience – are working-class autobiography. It seems to us that this elision of Williams's model of culture with a historian's notion of the documentary, and of *authenticity* is what produces that preoccupation in Left History of the 1970s with working-class autobiography, and the central question of who speaks for history. For the historian, it seems, sees culture as providing documentary evidence of group consciousness in the form of a *record* of individual testimony – culture *is* the collection of such materials, hitherto disregarded as irrelevant, or as insufficiently documentary. Whereas for Williams, the class-specificity of an individual's self-discovery and self-definition is the product of his engagement from a position of inequality with a *common culture* – class-consciousness is the specific shared ways in which the members of a class make general sense of their individual experiences.

We have suggested several times that Thompson's work was extremely influential (and deservedly so, in view of its originality) in redirecting and focusing historical studies on the Left. It is startling, therefore, to find how Thompson's thinking is poised on a knife-edge between historical studies and cultural studies, and how he relies at crucial points on formulations carried over from Williams's *Culture and Society*. We should recall that at crucial moments in *his* thinking, Williams similarly leans on historical studies, as shaped by Thompson. The two are, we are arguing, continuously in unacknowledged dialogue, the emphasis of one sometimes deflecting or colouring the argument of the other, so that the resulting treatment, looked at in the kind of detail we have attempted here, is surprisingly arcane. Thompson's account of historical class-consciousness is, in the end, esoteric of its very nature. However absorbing for the intellectual historian, excavating the intertwined strands of the literary and the historical within it, it ultimately carries as idiosyncratic a hallmark as does the equivalent formulation of 'culture and society' by Raymond Williams. But the connections established in what we are proposing as a New Left model for historical explanation (connections which amount, of course, to a theoretical underpinning, in spite of Thompson's claim to reject theory) have been sustained, submerged and unscrutinized, ever since. When we pass to the next generation of 'Thompsonian' Left historians it becomes evident that the moves we have seen Thompson making in his own work (from history to culture, from experience to moral realism) have had far-reaching consequences for historical studies.

In 1974, for example, Gareth Stedman Jones published an influential article in the *Journal of Social History* whose title, 'Working-class culture and working-class politics in London, 1870–1900: the remaking of a working class', clearly indicated an affiliation to Thompson's work. In his introduction to *Languages of Class*, in which this early essay is reprinted, he describes the relationship of this piece of work to Thompson's as follows:

> At this point, I was primarily interested, not in embarking upon a programme of empirical research, but rather in developing a theoretical framework within which to interpret the conflicts of the pre-1850 period. One way forward had been pioneered by Edward Thompson. His powerful and imaginative account of *The Making of the English Working Class* involved a considerable revision of orthodox Marxist assumptions about consciousness, the economy and the place of politics. Although sympathetic to the historical fruits of these revisions and heavily indebted at the time to his conception of 'culture', I continued to have reservations about his conception of historical method. My own predilection was towards a theoretical revision in a more structuralist direction and was inspired more by French than English currents of thinking. For me, the relationship of the historian to theory was not an external one – the attempted empirical validation of a pre-existing categorical currency (class consciousness, class struggle, labour aristocracy etc.) – but rather the location and construction of an invisible structure capable both of illuminating the direction of change on the surface and suggesting the limits within which it operated.[36]

Stedman Jones acknowledges an opposition here between his sympathy for the *kind* of account Thompson's historical method yields, and his reservations about the method *per se*. Unfortunately, it seems to us that in spite of Stedman Jones's purportedly discarding 'the attempted empirical validation of a pre-existing categorical currency (class consciousness, class struggle, labour aristocracy etc.)', his commitment to Thompson's conception of culture (his being 'heavily indebted at the time to [Thompson's] conception of "culture"') introduces a confusion into the heart of his own work. For 'culture' is already a category, defined by Thompson (with due indebtedness, as we have seen, to Williams) as part of the project to trace emerging class-consciousness, and in relation to the rest of the 'pre-existing categorical currency' Stedman Jones hopes to avoid.

Stedman Jones looked at the 'culture' proposed by Thompson as the source of early nineteenth-century working-class consciousness – Blake's 'Jerusalem', let's say – and it looked to him quite unlike twentieth-century 'working-class culture'. When Stedman Jones looks for political consciousness in the working-class culture of the twentieth century, he cannot find it, he can only find resistance to bourgeois *culture*, and he takes this as evidence that between the 1830s and the present day something about working-class consciousness, in its relationship to culture, *altered*. He takes it that the working classes, like their culture, lost the potential for class-based activism, settled into acceptance of their class role under capitalism. But in the work of the earlier generation of Left historians, as Williams observed (and we quoted above): 'The basis of a distinction between bourgeois and working-class culture is only secondarily in the field of intellectual and imaginative work, and even here it is complicated, as we have seen, by the common elements resting on a common language.' In their terms, Stedman Jones is looking at this secondary manifestation, and therefore finds conformity, not opposition: 'The crucial distinguishing element in English life since the Industrial Revolution is not language, not dress, not leisure – for these indeed will tend to uniformity.' It is in the social relations described as the ability to recognize themselves in dominant culture (according to the Thompson/Williams theory/model) that contemporary working-class consciousness is to be found: 'The crucial distinction is between alternative ideas of the nature of social relationship.'

Because of this initial difference in address to 'culture', what Stedman Jones was interested in doing was accounting for 'the gulf which separated the working class depicted in [Thompson's *The Making of the English Working Class*] from that existing in the twentieth century'. Specifically, he wanted to argue that an alteration in the form of the culture produced (or possibly reflected) a less combative set of attitudes amongst the working classes, a resignation and a capitulation to bourgeois ideals and aspirations. The picture Stedman Jones paints is of a distinctively twentieth-century working-class consciousness emerging out of the class-consciousness which was 'made' (according to Thompson) in the 1830s, and mapped by changes in the nature of working-class culture:[37]

> In this paper, I shall attempt – very tentatively – to trace the conditions of emergence of a new working-class culture in London and to delineate its characteristic institutions and ideology. . . . I hope to explain the emergence of a working-class culture which showed itself staunchly impervious to middle-class attempts to guide it, but yet whose prevailing tone was not one of political combativity, but of an enclosed and defensive conservatism. In this way I hope to open up a different line of approach to the problem of London politics in the age of imperialism and to go a little way towards reconciling the cultural, economic and political history of the working class.[38]

Working-class culture, by consciously developing so as to be 'staunchly impervious' to middle-class pressures upon it, proceeded by consolidation, and lost its function as a source of politicized consciousness (so Stedman Jones's argument goes). There is much of interest and value in Stedman Jones's exploration of working-class organizations in the latter decades of the nineteenth century in this article, but the point we are focusing on is that *culture* here has altered its meaning, and has become that body of 'recreational' activities (including artistic production) which recognizably belongs to one social group in particular. Blake's 'Jerusalem' did not embody a working-class way of life, it offered a set of ideals (according to Thompson) to give value to that way of life. By contrast, music-hall – the form of specifically 'working-class' culture Stedman Jones selects for close inspection – enacts features of a recognizably class-based way of living – cloth caps, cockney accents and attitudes, mother-in-law jokes, jingoism, etc.

Here we have lost the valuable tension (intrinsic to the theory) between working-class consciousness and 'culture', in favour of something called 'working-class culture'; in the 1830s, apparently, this 'working-class culture' facilitated political confrontation, but by the end of the century its tone was that of 'an enclosed and defensive conservatism'. For this working class 'Jerusalem' is sung 'not as a battle-cry but as a hymn'; this working class's culture is an escape from political reality, not the means of galvanizing itself towards change, supporting and confirming a distinctive 'way of struggle'. This working class goes to the music-hall to preserve an authentic way of life for itself, to refuse middle-class values, to insist on its own distinctiveness (but *within* the existing class-hierarchy).

Stedman Jones is not looking at the same 'culture' that Thompson (and Williams) looked at, we are arguing. He is not looking at the same relationship between a repository of values for the whole community, addressed differently by distinctive groups within it, and the class-consciousness which enables political change. Hence the contradiction between culture as a source of political awareness (Thompson's model – the making of the English working class) and culture as a strongly conservative force as it reflects the taste, and meets the recreational requirements of 'local' groups. Stedman Jones struggles with the problem of whether his London working-class culture is typical of working-class culture as a whole, and this is not surprising. If culture reflects local detail, in what sense is it generally typical? The whole movement is towards local history, the ordinary, a kind of authenticity which is particular, peculiar, but not in a way which is in any obvious sense generalizable as a political force.

The conclusion of Stedman Jones's article brings his argument directly round to the Labour movement, which is probably why it has taken our own interest. In many ways Stedman Jones's objective is our own – to try to come to terms with a sense of the Labour movement as backward looking, as built upon the values of a defensive conservatism. According to Stedman Jones, the self-parodying, nostalgic modes of music hall reveal a shift in working-class consciousness which is also a drift away from confrontational politics on the part of the Labour movement:

> If the 'making of the English working class' took place in the 1790-1830 period, something akin to a remaking of the working class took place in the years between 1870 and 1900. For much of the cluster of 'traditional' working-class attitudes analysed by contemporary sociologists and literary critics dates, not from the first third, but from the last third of the nineteenth century. This remaking process did not obliterate the legacy of that first formative phase of working-class history, so well described by

Edward Thompson. But it did transform its meaning. In the realm of working-class ideology, a second formative layer of historical experience was superimposed upon the first, thereby colouring the first in the light of its own changed horizons of possibility. The struggles of the first half of the century were not forgotten, but they were recalled selectively and reinterpreted. The solidarity and organizational strength achieved in social struggles were channelled into trade union activity and eventually into a political party based upon that activity and its goals. The distinctiveness of a working-class way of life was enormously accentuated. Its separateness and impermeability were now reflected in a dense and inward-looking culture, whose effect was both to emphasize the distance of the working class from the classes above it and to articulate its position within an apparently permanent social hierarchy. The growth of trade unionism on the one hand and the new working-class culture on the other were not contradictory but interrelated phenomena.[39]

It is undoubtedly the case that 'the growth of trade unionism on the one hand and the new working-class culture on the other were . . . interrelated phenomena'; but the reinterpretation and transformation of the meaning of working-class consciousness – its reduction from a consciousness of a shared set of values to a shared nostalgia, tastes, and pleasures – is inadvertently Stedman Jones's. His reframing of the issues, however, is also importantly symptomatic of a general failure on the part of the Left to address the way in which a peculiarly English sensibility which developed in the third quarter of the nineteenth century (the period on which Stedman Jones focuses, and the period of that particular sensibility of Morris's so cherished by Thompson in his early work) became accepted as the definitive form of English working-class consciousness, instead of the shaping but constantly changing force it had (as originally developed in Left theory) been intended to be.

We will come back to this larger theme in our last chapter. For the moment we need to carry our argument back to autobiography, and working-class authenticity as the focus for Left historical effort and attention in the 1970s. If we return to our opening debate amongst historians of working-class autobiography, we should now be able to see that the argument over the significance of autobiography for history – the way in which that argument goes off in two apparently opposed directions – is directly attributable to that fracture within Thompson's account between document and narrative, historical studies and cultural studies, which the term 'culture' gives the illusion of mending. When Yeo regards the terms 'autobiographical mode' and 'working-class autobiography' as interchangeable, and writes that 'worker writing and community publishing has a lot to teach historians', he assumes the Thompson model. 'Autobiography' is only of interest to the historian insofar as it provides evidence, not for individual experience and local detail, but as the articulation of shared class-consciousness in terms of the historically current cultural forms (and that is *only* working-class consciousness). When Jerry White rejects autobiography as local and parochial, as insufficiently objective for the historian, he is acknowledging the intrusion of culture in the formation of the individual autobiographical account, and rejecting (as a historian) the claim that one could excavate something general, something more like the historically documentary from within such narratives. But the very existence of such a debate suggests that the local historians as a group have lost sight of the original justification for claiming working-class autobiography as a source of historical authenticity – a justification which was strenuously theoretical, and depended on a particular version of 'culture'. Likewise, the pronouncements of the Birmingham Popular Memory Group suggest that they have themselves forgotten the original, political justification for their enterprise: 'Oral history and popular autobiography are forms which systematically individualize: yet an historically-informed political knowledge requires a much broader sense of social context.' It was the interplay, the theoretical to-and-fro between individual statement and generalized consciousness which led the New Left historians to turn to oral history and autobiography in the first place. The formulation offered by Ken Worpole, which heads the present chapter, manages still to hold this configuration steady – as a theoretical configuration which is intended to inform a political practice:

> The autobiographical mode, widely espoused by the local history projects, is the mode of the long revolution, slower, acknowledging difficulty, mixing occasional insights into the prime causes and determinants of life – homelessness, redundancy – with experiences of sudden bereavement, a loving relationship, mental breakdown in the family, the party that lasted for three days, the failed attempt to emigrate. And who is to say that the latter experiences do not help us to clarify the complexity of the revolution we have ahead of us?

We said early on in this chapter that the present argument was in a sense a doubling back, that it has to be set alongside that developing insistence on the unconscious within a feminism which had started out as Marxist, and within a Left feminist history. We have now reached the point where it should be possible to see how closely the argument about 'local history' and 'personal history' in general matches that which we saw going on amongst feminist historians in *History Workshop* at the end of the last chapter. Alexander and Taylor, in particular, wanted to argue that there was no evidence of women's lived experience in a form available to the historian, even if she *is* a feminist historian. There is nothing, in other words, which matches that version of 'autobiography' to which the Left historian gives his attention in the search for working-class consciousness in history. But (in the wake of Juliet Mitchell) *they* propose making up for this absence of evidence of working-class women's consciousness by turning to the *unconscious*: 'Their strategy on behalf of a specifically feminist history is to shift methodological ground to that of psychoanalysis, whose methodology is to detect (and provide therapy for) contradictions in the social in the disturbed testimony of the individual subject (most particularly, in the voice of the female hysteric).'[40]

We end this chapter by suggesting that both the local historians' interest in autobiography, and the feminist historians' search for a historical authenticity gendered female, end in the same kind of impasse – that local history's commitment to 'personal history' (the confessional) comes to match feminist history's commitment to 'case history' (the psychoanalytical). For the question 'who speaks for history?' has turned out to be anything but anodyne. Once the connection with a New Left version of historical explanation is lost sight of – and we are claiming that it *has* been lost sight of by social and local historians, and that the dispute over the authenticity of autobiography as history confirms this – then the theoretical value of the individual, autobiographical mode is lost, and its importance for a non-elite history becomes, apparently, simply its *ordinariness*. Meanwhile, feminist historians assume that they are looking in history for 'ordinary' female *subjectivity*, on the strength of a commitment by a particular section of feminist theory to the unconscious.

As we have found before, an account which can be held steady in spite of its growing theoretical difficulties in relation to men in history (for whom, we have argued, the account was originally, unreflectively designed) tends to fail dramatically and obviously when we come to the historian's treatment of a woman. It is in the context of historical treatment of working *women*'s autobiography that the problems latent in this second-generation Left historical approach surface most clearly. The example we take here is one which has gained some prominence in women's history courses, the 'autobiography' of Hannah Cullwick.[41]

Here is how the title-page blurb introduces Hannah Cullwick and her diary, in the Virago edition edited by Liz Stanley:

> Hannah Cullwick was born in Shifnal, Shropshire in 1833, the daughter of a housemaid and a saddler. She began work at the age of eight when she went to her 'petty place' to learn the skills of domestic service: a lower servant for most of her life, she was maid-of-all-work, but also pot-girl, cook, housemaid, char and housekeeper. In 1854 she met Arthur Munby (1828-1910), 'man of two worlds', an upper-class author and poet, with a lifelong obsession with lower-class women. For the next eighteen years they conducted a secret courtship and during those years Hannah wrote her diaries – seventeen in all. She did so at her 'Massa''s behest in order to keep him in touch with her daily drudgery, every detail of which he sought from her.
>
> At the time of their marriage (which was to last for the next thirty-six years) in 1873 the diaries ceased.[42]

In spite of the curious circumstances surrounding the diary, detailed here – the fact that they were written at the behest of her 'Massa', an upper-class author 'with a lifelong obsession with lower-class women', 'in order to keep him in touch with her daily drudgery, every detail of which he sought from her' – Stanley's introduction stresses above all the *ordinariness* of Cullwick and her autobiography:

> This book is concerned with the life and writings of a woman who was never famous, indeed who was born, lived, wrote and died in total obscurity. Her name was Hannah Cullwick and she wrote diaries which bring home to us with a quite unique freshness and immediacy what it meant to live and work as a lower-class woman 'in service' in early and middle Victorian England. . . . For me, it is precisely her 'ordinariness' that makes Hannah so 'extra-ordinary'. She is an ordinary lower-class woman of the Victorian

period; but her life, and her working life, is fully documented. The result is not only that she is 'the most thoroughly documented housemaid of the Victorian age', but also the most thoroughly documented, thoroughly ordinary working-class woman of a period of which we still know all too little.[43]

In the light of the present chapter, this aspiration to find the 'most thoroughly documented, thoroughly ordinary working-class woman' appears to be directly in line with the local history project, and with that second-generation Left historian's pursuit of a first-person account which embodies working-class consciousness: 'The "maid-of-all-work" was literally that and represented the most common form of female service. Hannah's writings therefore provide us with a unique insight into the working lives of this most substantial group of Victorian working women.'[44] So Cullwick's diaries might be taken as 'individual testimony' which could yield the historian a generalized sense of working-class consciousness in the second half of the nineteenth century. And indeed, Stanley picks out in her introduction the strong theme of 'service' in Cullwick's diaries – a theme which Williams had drawn attention to as particularly significant in the late-nineteenth-century relationship of working-class consciousness to culture:

> Hannah enjoyed physical labour, feeling and using her considerable bodily strength and exercising the skills of her trade. And on this she said, 'They was often wondering at me being so big & strong & when I lifted anything very heavy they'd say, "Why Hannah carries it in one hand & I couldn't do it wi' two!" . . . & of course there *is* a difference . . . Servants may feel it sharply & sometimes I believe, but it's best not to be delicate, nor mind what work we do so as it's honest . . . but keeping a soft & tender heart all the while'. This was coupled with Hannah's analysis of 'service' and the role that this played in her religious beliefs, for she saw servitude as a Christian duty and ladyhood as entailing a lack of proper humility. She said of ladies and gentlemen, that 'I don't envy 'em at all, for if I was a lady & had such a lot o' fine things, I think I should be afraid I was never humble enough in God's sight'.[45]

The 'historical evidence' Cullwick's diaries provide of the way she internalizes the idea of 'service' to give value to the menial activities she carries out from her wholly subordinate social position (both as general maidservant, and as 'slave' or 'drudge' to Munby's 'Massa') seems interestingly to confirm Williams's observations about 'service', and its prominent place in bourgeois culture, in *Culture and Society*.[46] Williams contrasts the working-class ethic of 'solidarity' with the bourgeois idea of 'service', to argue that whilst both are notionally opposed to 'liberal individualism', the latter provides no practical basis for an active working-class consciousness:

> The idea of service, ultimately, is no substitute for the idea of active mutual responsibility, which is the other version of community. Few men [sic] can give of themselves as servants; it is the reduction of men to a function. Further, the servant, if he is to be a good servant, can never really question the order of things; his sense of authority is too strong. Yet the existing order is in fact subject to almost overwhelming pressures. The break through, into what together we want to make of our lives, will need qualities which the idea of service not only fails to provide, but, in its limitation of our minds, actively harms.[47]

Cullwick's diaries are available for analysis to show how, historically, the 'idea of service' 'actively harms' the working-class woman's ability to resist her subordinate position in her work and personal relations. But that is not what Stanley chooses to look at, nor does she have very much to say at all, in her introduction, about those extensive portions of the diaries which document Cullwick's work, her working conditions, and Victorian labour relations in general. Stanley sets out instead to retrieve Cullwick's individual selfhood from the diaries, and she does so by concentrating on the most problematic material in the diaries, that concerned with her personal relationship with Munby. In other words, in practice, Stanley follows the feminist historians we looked at in Chapter 4, in exploring Cullwick's *unconscious*, to retrieve the voice of the 'authentic' Cullwick, silenced by history, or ventriloquized by Munby and his male biographers. Her task, reiterated throughout the explanatory material which accompanies the transcriptions of the diaries, is to retrieve Cullwick 'as she saw herself', rather than 'as Munby saw her'.

It is, in the light of Chapter 4, predictable and revealing that Stanley should turn away from Cullwick, working woman, and towards Cullwick, slave, lover, and wife of Munby, in search of

Cullwick's 'real' identity in history. And it is certainly no straightforward matter to excavate the authentic subjecthood of Hannah Cullwick from the narrative of her relations with Munby as that is produced (for Munby) in her diaries. There are, as Stanley puts it, aspects of Cullwick's relationship with Munby which 'might shock, startle or offend some people on moral or political grounds':

> For years up until their marriage Hannah wore a padlock and chain around her neck, to which only Munby had the key. Soon after they met she began to call him 'Massa', which both of them took to be the black slave pronunciation of 'master', to signify that her primary servitude was to him. During the early part of their relationship she 'blacked up' by covering herself in black lead, the better to show herself his slave, in mimicry of the so-called 'nigger troupes' that roamed London with a multitude of other street entertainments. On occasions she licked his boots. She swept chimneys and cleaned front steps for him. She only rarely ate meals in his presence, waited on him and washed his feet.[48]

Inevitably Stanley is drawn into the kinds of formulation which gave us trouble in Chapter 4: 'The paradox that exists here is that the drudgery that was everyday life for the maid-of-all-work also in a sense liberated her. . . . For the Victorians, "femininity" demanded "appropriate" behaviours, aptitudes, activities and styles of dress; and failure to display these led to the withdrawal of approbation and so in a sense unsexed a woman.'[49] By going out 'in her dirt', for instance, so as to appear sexually enticing to Munby, Cullwick is supposedly able to liberate herself from the constraints of bourgeois Victorian women's lives.[50] Or, Stanley imputes agency to Cullwick within the terms of the sexual situation described in the diaries:

> I believe that Hannah used and encouraged Munby's needs and obsessions – with dirt and squalor, subservience and mastery, whiteness and darkness – to establish and maintain their relationship. In other words, she used 'powerlessness' to achieve 'power' over him so as to confirm his need for her and thus the relationship; for there was little else that could have bound him to her in any permanent fashion . . . power was distributed in many complex and changing ways between them.[51]

It ought to be clear, we believe, that in this account of the personal relations of a 'thoroughly ordinary working-woman', the pursuit of a distinctive working-class consciousness gendered female has collapsed into a confused articulation of a pointedly individualized selfhood, its intimacies and dependencies. Our own firm belief is that this is certainly not the path we should follow in the search for a Left account of non-elite women in history, that the enterprise has somehow broken up on the shoals of an individual self-consciousness which is immune to change, and politically unhelpful, both in terms of class and of gender.

Chapter Six

Culture in the working classroom
'There's no place like home'

In a wider context there was the humanism of Raymond Williams, and the concerns of Richard Hoggart and Stuart Hall. Generously interpreted, psychological understanding of fictional characters fitted in there, too.

(Juliet Mitchell, 1984)[1]

British culture as it exists today is a profound obstacle to revolutionary politics. What is meant by culture here? A preliminary delimitation is essential. We are not concerned with the anthropological conception of culture, as the sum of social customs and symbols in a given society. The generalization of this use of the term characterized the Left in the fifties, and was responsible for some important insights into British society: this was the moment of Richard Hoggart's *Uses of Literacy*. But this usage also blurred the specificity of the superstructural complex which is a society's original thought and art.

(Perry Anderson, 1968)[2]

In the mid-1950s Richard Hoggart's attitude to Marxism was one of explicit hostility, Raymond Williams's was one of active critique, Stuart Hall's (I would surmise) was one of sceptical ambivalence, whereas, from 1956 onwards, the *Reasoner* group, with which was associated, closely or loosely, a number of Marxist historians . . . this group was attempting to defend, re-examine and extend the Marxist tradition at a time of political and theoretical disaster.

I am not saying that we were right, and that Hoggart or Raymond Williams or Stuart Hall were wrong. I am not trying to fight out old fraternal battles or differences over again. It may well be that we old Marxists at that time had got into ruts, and that Hoggart, Williams or Hall, running free on the surrounding terrain [the Moors?], helped to tow us out.

(E. P. Thompson, 1979)[3]

R.W.: I'm glad that at last we've managed to meet. Since *The Uses of Literacy* and *Culture and Society* came out, many people have assumed that we knew each other well, though in fact I think it's been no more than exchanging perhaps half a dozen letters in the last twelve years, none of them, it seems, while the books were being written. Of course it's natural that the two books should have been compared and connected, but such relationships as there are have come out of the general situation, and not from our knowing each other.

(transcript of a recorded conversation between Richard Hoggart and Raymond Williams, from the opening issue of *New Left Review*, 1960)[4]

In this chapter we try to bring the parallel strands of the last two chapters together. We want to argue that feminism's move from class history to 'case history', and Left history's move from class history to 'personal history' have played a major part in developments within Left education theory, inadvertently privileging individual self-hood in the classroom in the name of class-consciousness. In order to do so, we bring into the story Richard Hoggart (who as Thompson reminds us, wasn't even a Marxist, was actively hostile to Marxism), because the Left in the 1960s seemed so sure that Williams's *Culture and Society* and Hoggart's *The Uses of Literacy* were connected, and that both were crucial for an authentically Left educational strategy. Much of this chapter will be trying to sort out why this is the case – why whenever in the 1960s the Left turned its attention to education it invoked Richard Hoggart, and *The Uses of Literacy* (but *The Uses of Literacy* is hardly about education at all, as we shall see), and why at the same time it assumed Williams's version of culture as crucial to the educational debate. For, as Thompson says, it does seem in some important sense to have been the case that Hoggart and Williams (and Hall, but we can't deal in detail with everyone) helped to 'tow out' culture-committed Marxists from negative critique of the contemporary situation into active Left involvement with reform in the classroom.[5]

In 1968 Perry Anderson saw 'British culture' as 'a profound

obstacle to revolutionary politics'. His denunciation of the Old Left (in particular E. P. Thompson) was a denunciation of their assumption of, and continuing commitment to, British culture (we traced that argument in detail in Chapter 2). Anderson's version of the stranglehold of 'culture' on British thought was couched, in this crucial article, in terms of the British educational system: its failure to provide a vantage point (sociology) from which the culture which saturated the society as a whole could be scrutinized and dismantled. And here (but as far as we can see, nowhere else in his writing) he takes Richard Hoggart as representative of the 1950s Left as a whole, and singles him out as the member of the 'culture-committed' group who was nevertheless responsible for some 'important insights'.

At the very moment at which Anderson was identifying 'culture' as the impediment to revolutionary politics, Raymond Williams was representing it as a crucial terrain on which the battle lines for class struggle were drawn up:

Culture was the way in which the process of education, the experience of literature, and – for someone moving out of a working-class family to a higher education – inequality, came through. What other people, in different situations, might experience more directly as economic or political inequality, was naturally experienced, from my own route, as primarily an inequality of culture: an inequality which was also, in an obvious sense, an uncommunity. This is, I think, still the most important way to follow the argument about culture, because everywhere, but very specifically in England, culture is one way in which class, the fact of major divisions between men, shows itself.[6]

Here Williams attaches political importance to his own *experience* of inequality in relation to culture, and identifies class inequality with that feeling of exclusion in relation to [high] culture ('the process of education, the experience of literature'): 'Everywhere, but very specifically in England, culture is one way in which class, the fact of major divisions between men, shows itself.' So that, by implication, one way of *altering* that class inequality, and that 'uncommunity', is to tackle it within education (by means of that 'oppositional' which *Culture and Society* was looking for).

It is instructive here to register how close this account of an experience of inequality in culture, and then the turning to education as the means of change, lies to Leavis's (contemporary) position, as Williams (as we saw in Chapter 2) freely acknowledges:

> The immense attraction of Leavis lay in his cultural radicalism, quite clearly.
> Finally, there was Leavis's great stress on education. He would always emphasize that there was an enormous educational job to be done. Of course, he defined it in his own terms. But the emphasis itself seemed completely right to me.[7]

The important thing for the present discussion is that Williams first puts Leavis in, and then ostentatiously takes him out – shifts the discussion away from him, once the point has been taken – and so do we.[8] It is important to recognize that the key terms of the Hoggart/Williams-inspired educational debate are 'culture' and 'community', and that these are also Leavis's pivotal terms for education. We shall argue, as we argued about Thompson in Chapter 3, that Hoggart – outside the immediate circle of Leavis's influence – fails to distinguish his version of 'culture' and 'community' from Leavis's, with considerable consequences.[9]

And perhaps Williams recognizes the Leavis link when (in that interview recorded in the first issue of *New Left Review*) he says that 'it's natural that [*Culture and Society* and *The Uses of Literacy*] should have been compared and connected, but such relationships as there are have come out of the general situation, and not from our knowing each other'. 'Culture' and 'community' are the currency of contemporary educational debate and they are shared terms in those two works (the relationship comes out of the general situation). For Williams those terms point directly to class, and inequality (in careful contradistinction to Leavis). Insofar as Hoggart may be said to be aware of his terms as depending on a prior set of theoretical assumptions, 'community' is taken in Leavis's sense of a lost 'organic community', and 'culture' as that high ideal whose dissipation and disintegration is a feature of the mechanized industrial city. As Leavis put it:

> What has disintegrated – this is the point – is not merely 'bourgeois' or 'capitalist' civilization; it is the organic community. Instead of the rural community and the town-community we have, almost universally, suburbanism. . . . The organic community has virtually disappeared, and with it the only basis for a genuine

national culture; so nearly disappeared that when one speaks of the old popular culture that existed in innumerable local variations people cannot grasp what one means. . . . The memory of the old order, the old ways of life, must be the chief hint for, the directing incitement towards, a new, if ever there is to be a new.[10]

The conservatism of this version of culture and community is explicit. But, as we shall see, Left educational theory in the 1960s somehow contrived to overlay Hoggart with Williams, so as to claim the Hoggart/Leavis version of 'cultural radicalism' (which Williams had noted) as their own. In other words, by using Hoggart as their justification for a particular set of usages (which include 'community', and 'culture'), educationalists produced a programme (and a curriculum) for building and amplifying a distinctive class-consciousness for the individual working-class child, by supporting a particular kind of engagement with high culture. Hoggart was the pivotal text, guaranteeing (apparently) the progressiveness of this undertaking (although on the face of it it might as well be taken as a training in bourgeois individualism).

The crucial issue is the identification of individualized class-consciousness, as opposed to traditional individualism, and everywhere in the Left's encounter with Hoggart this problem is in evidence. In that recorded first encounter which launched *New Left Review*, Raymond Williams talked to Richard Hoggart about what it meant for them both to be working class, and there is a strong sense in the discussion (their first public encounter) that he was trying to provide an account of class-consciousness and culture which they would both be able to share. Not surprisingly, the conversation is somehow blurred, and above all, is strikingly anecdotal – because although Hoggart and Williams both use the terms (culture, community) of a 'general situation', what they actually have in common is a strongly felt need to identify their own individual past as working-class. And they struggle to find common ground in their own personal experience – that is, somewhere where they can place an 'oppositional' to their (evidently shared) educational opportunities, and experiences of public life as professional educators.

We find Williams, in dialogue with Hoggart, struggling to sustain a tension between individual lived experience (his own and Hoggart's autobiographies) and working-class consciousness. Hoggart, on the other hand, seems content from the outset to regard the project as that of discovering working-class authenticity – of producing himself and Williams as the subjects of working-class autobiography. And it is apparent from the outset that such a project is intimately related to Hoggart's intellectual undertaking in *The Uses of Literacy*:

> *The Uses of Literacy* was originally finished in the summer of 1955. . . . I had begun in 1952 too [The year Williams began *Culture and Society*], by writing one chapter which doesn't appear. I was thinking of something quite simple in scope and size – a series of critical essays on popular literature. Soon I began to feel that I wanted to relate this material to the day-to-day experience of people. After this a strange thing happened . . . things I'd been writing since 1946 (bits of a novel and some unconnected descriptive pieces) began to fall into place in the new book.[11]

In its incorporation of 'bits of a novel and some unconnected descriptive pieces' this is already interestingly unreflective when contrasted with the way in which Williams immediately tackles that idea of a grounding 'day-to-day experience of people':

> It seemed to me I had to try to go back over the tradition, to look at it again and get it into relation with my own experience, to see the way the intellectual tradition stood in the pattern of my own growing-up. As I saw the cultural tradition then, it was mainly Coleridge, Arnold, Leavis and the Marxists, and the development, really, was a discovery of relationships inside the tradition, and also a discovery of other relationships: Cobbett and Morris, for example, who brought in parts of my experience that had been separate before. Getting the tradition right was getting myself right, and that meant changing both myself and the usual version of the tradition. I think this is one of the problems we're both conscious of: moving out of a working-class home into an academic curriculum, absorbing it first and then, later, trying to get the two experiences into relation.[12]

Here is that insistence on individual experience as standing at the intersection of a set of relations – relations inside the 'tradition' (in the Arnoldian, cultural sense), 'other relationships' which 'brought in parts of [his] experience that had been separate before'. And finally, 'getting the tradition right was getting myself right': a self-consciousness about the need to alter, to intervene and shape, from that initial position of inequality in relation to high culture. Where Hoggart's instinct appears to be to consolidate what he can value from his specifically *working-class* culture (the way of life), Williams is to alter, to change; but for both the route is through education: 'I think this is one of the problems we're both conscious of: moving out of a working-class home into an academic curriculum, absorbing it first and then, later, trying to get the two experiences into relation.'[13]

Early on in the conversation, Williams draws attention to their 'very different ways of life', and asks Hoggart to look at Williams's village Wales, while he, Williams, looks at Hoggart's industrial city of Leeds: 'I'd like you to look at Pandy and I at Hunslet.'[14] In practice, though, Hoggart tends to talk about Leeds, and Williams talks about Wales, and the conversation does indeed highlight the differences of which Williams has spoken – 'very different ways of life'. At one point, while Williams is describing his father's occupation as signalman and his perceived status of their family *vis-à-vis* poverty, Hoggart intervenes briefly to say, 'I know we used to look up to railwaymen and policemen.' Williams agrees – 'we weren't poor' – and shifts the argument onto class-consciousness – the 'more complicated' argument about the consciousness of being working class.

Hoggart maintains that industrial Leeds lacked 'a kind of organic quality', which he imagines to be a feature of working-class life in rural Wales, but he identifies a persisting sense of community in the 'connections' between working-class men and their 'neighbourhood':

> Among working-people you had extended families, often overlapping; and particular neighbourhood loyalties; and you had distinctions between say the transport men, the heavy engineering men, those who laboured for the Corporation and so on and so on. The distinctions were very fine and very complicated. But still you could see first this large rough distinction – that industrially the area was a block, or a pool, of general labour for the city's industries – the human equivalent of the private reservoirs at the side of some of the big works. In our area there were a lot of men who hadn't served an apprenticeship, who weren't skilled workers – or not really skilled – but who could turn their hands to a number of jobs within related heavy industries. They felt two main kinds of connections, with their neighbourhood and with the industries they worked in; but the neighbourhood connections were stronger for most.[15]

Williams is also clear that 'ordinary working-class life' supports a 'sense of community', but he represents this sense of community as alive and well, and as coming fundamentally from the place of work:

> The most difficult bit of theory, that I think both of us have been trying to get at, is what relation there is between kinds of community, that we call working-class, and the high working-class tradition, leading to democracy, solidarity in the unions, socialism. As I saw it, this came from the place of work: in my village, the railway. I suppose this is always likely to be so. But is it the case that the high tradition is strongest where there are certain kinds of community: the mining villages, for example? To what extent can we establish a relation between given kinds of working-class community and what we call working-class consciousness in the sense of the Labour movement? . . . All I'd say is that certain major principles, that matter for our future, have in fact come out of the high working-class tradition, supported by many aspects of working-class life. I mean the sense of community, of equality, of genuine mutual respect: the sense, too, of fairness, when the humanity of everyone in this society is taken as basic, and must not be outraged by any kind of exploitation.[16]

'To what extent can we establish a relation between given kinds of working-class community and what we call working-class consciousness in the sense of the Labour movement?' Williams asks, and the question is, for him, a directly political one. In our attempt to unravel that perceived close relationship between Williams's *Culture and Society* and Hoggart's *The Uses of Literacy*, Hoggart's reluctance to concede that 'a sense of community' has a bearing on political consciousness, in this dialogue is instructive. Hoggart's 'sense of community' exists *alongside* the place of work, and is distinct from any political consciousness to be found in the workplace: 'They felt two main kinds of connections, with their neighbourhood and with the industries they worked in; but the neighbourhood connections were stronger for most.' And this leads Hoggart to lay crucial emphasis here (as he does throughout *The Uses of Literacy*) on the working-class *family* as the source for authentic working-class values – somewhat in desperation, at what he sees as the disintegration of working-class solidarity in the public domain:

Today people are moving around more; many of the old areas are being split up; new industries and new forms of industry are recruiting people from all over, offering good wages and a much more fluid range of opportunities. What we want to know is what replaces the old channels by which political consciousness expressed itself.[17]

Lamenting the loss of working-class solidarity (which he appears to label as 'political consciousness' almost accidentally, since his commitment is apparently in a very broad sense to 'working class' as an authentic category of experience) through 'the old channels', Hoggart naturally (but perhaps not consciously) appeals to a Leavisite model of culture and community – a current and available source both for a vocabulary of values and for a justificatory nostalgia, which locates those values in cohesive pre-industrial units, remote from urban centres and their attendant corruptions (mass communications and consumerism).[18]

In one of the quotations at the beginning of this chapter we saw Anderson arguing that a particular version of culture produced in the 1950s – and he names *The Uses of Literacy* – has its virtues, but that it blurred the critique of culture as part of society's 'superstructural complex'. What we saw too, in the debate between the Old Left and the New Left in our Chapter 2, is that the 'stranglehold' of culture on the Old Left meant that even the history of E. P. Thompson failed to escape (or even to recognize) a particularly damaging affinity with Leavis in producing and elaborating a narrative of moral realism. It is not so much that Leavis's use of 'culture' and 'community' is intrinsically conservative, as the *fact* that it is possible to elide a nostalgic, autobiographical mode with an evaluative mode which claims explicitly radical origins and goals, which causes the damage. Anderson barely pauses on the actual case of Hoggart, but what he does do (as we have seen him do before) is to detect a problem, and to put his finger on the fact that Hoggart is at its crux – is somehow peculiarly representative of the problem.

We can begin to see that in Hoggart's desire to retrieve an identity-forming, politically cohesive, authentic working-class experience he resorts to a version of the moral realist narrative which is validated by its apparent compatibility with a contemporary Left version of history. As he mobilizes his personal history – his autobiography –, as part of an argument about *education*, this has consequences which go beyond narrative – which make particular versions of 'culture' and 'community' into models (goals, aspirations) towards which a Left educational strategy should be aimed (just as Leavis's evaluative language also envisages and is linked to particular educational objectives).

As we argue in both Chapters 2 and 3, it is in 'the family' that we can see where models of history and class-consciousness are skewed. For Hoggart, the attachment to family is particularly strong and revealing. In Part One of *The Uses of Literacy* he maps his sense of an 'older order' of the working class around a version of the family in which 'There's no place like Home', and in which Mother, Father, and the Neighbourhood have a solid place. Tracing and evaluating working-class home life from 'personal experience', Hoggart is drawing on memories of twenty years earlier (and inevitably, drawing on the memory of the 'older order' – Leavis's phrase – which carries its own nostalgia), but there is something rather poignant in his admission that his own mother died when her children were infants, and that, in the strict sense, Hoggart did not have the model which he is describing, with Mother as the centre. In other words, received cultural versions of the (morally good) family already shape his account. Without making too much of this individual re-drawing of personal experience, we suggest that Hoggart is here already appealing to a version of the family recognizably related to the one we scrutinized in Orwell in Chapter 1, or at least, with similar problems.

> This is in many respects a good and comely life, one founded on care, affection, a sense of the small group if not of the individual. It is elaborate and disorderly and yet sober: it is not chintzy or kittenish or whimsical or 'feminised'. The father is part of the inner life of the home, not someone who spends most of his time miles away earning the money to keep the establishment going: the mother is the working-centre, always with too much to do and with her thoughts revolving almost entirely around the life of this family room (bedrooms are simply places you sleep in). Her 'one hope', as she puts it, is that her daughters and sons will 'soon find a nice lad or lass and make homes of their own'.[19]

In Orwell, too, home life falls 'into sane and comely shape',[20] and as Bea Campbell points out in *Wigan Pier Revisited*, neither Orwell nor Hoggart is concerned to address 'the brutality of that "comely" place', 'the inequalities inscribed in the working-class household'.[21] Hoggart's particular usage of the family – in the above passage divorcing the father from his work-place (and thereby refusing any acknowledgement of the economic relations of the family) and conflating the mother with work ('the working-centre') as if she were a machine rather than a worker – functions to dislocate class from any economic and industrial struggle, and to personalize class history. In family, he finds 'a sense of the small group if not of the individual', and values are conferred on that small group, that set of individuals, via a 'domestic past'.[22]

Hoggart's use of history, therefore, is different from that of E. P. Thompson, in that, for Hoggart, history is personal memory of a domestic past, whereas for Thompson, that same or similar domestic past is not actually history, but functions to supply value to the central figures, the William Morrises, of history. Both lean on the 'organic community' (and hence, at least indirectly, on Leavis); in the Hoggart account this comes increasingly to look as if it is the same thing as this nostalgic domestic past. But the distinction between the two was methodologically vital in the formation both of Williams's and Thompson's versions of 'lived experience' as a cornerstone of authentic class-consciousness. By collapsing 'lived experience' into a personal domestic past Hoggart inadvertently (but perhaps predictably) loses the tension necessary for a politicized account of the relationship between culture and the working class.[23] Anderson had recognized that there was something about 1950s social-anthropological accounts which failed to engage the critique of culture, but the 'personal experience' quality of Hoggart's *The Uses of Literacy* led him nevertheless to concede that he had 'some important insights' – the important insights which come from *being* working-class, but as we know perfectly well (away from this seductive focus on family) such insights would need to be 'placed' in a theoretical framework, in ways in which Hoggart's are not (in spite of the claim that terms like 'culture' and 'community' apparently make). Moreover, we argue that this presenting of 'personal history' (and the personal history only of the working-class boy) as class history, gave an intensely misleading map to educators, particularly as it was coaxed into a mesh with Raymond Williams's oppositional model of culture.

We can now name the problem. Hoggart is giving a particular profile to *self*-consciousness as class-consciousness (the self as the personal constituted within the familial of the nostalgic domestic past – community *as* this concept of the personal in past time). We shall argue later in this chapter that part of the problem, and a particular problem for girls for reasons that we explored in Chapter 4, is that this version of the self then yields a therapeutic model to educators (class history to case history). But for the moment we are showing the problem in Hoggart, to see why educators were able to turn to that model.

The version of political consciousness which Hoggart produces in *The Uses of Literacy* is sharply focused in the section of the book which deals with 'the scholarship boy' – 'a note on the uprooted and the anxious' (and that notion of anxiety already apparently justifies therapeutic intervention). In Hoggart's account, the working-class scholarship boy at the grammar school is in danger of having lost his own class-consciousness and identification with the working class, without having found an entry into the middle class. Strikingly enough, the chapter ends, not with an appeal to 'the uprooted and anxious' to become oppositional (to join the Labour Party or to participate in student activism?), but with marriage guidance and the benefits of family life:

> Beneath their apparent cynicism and self-pity is a deep sense of being lost, without purpose and with the will sapped. It sometimes seems to me that the situation is most difficult during their twenties, when the most strenuous search for cultural and intellectual satisfactions which are rarely gained takes place. There is usually a change after the first few years of marriage. But at first, and for a year or two, they have a trapped look, as though they have, by marrying, been guilty of a bourgeois weakness and, worse, allowed themselves to be caught, to betray their freedom. The climate of the time, as they apprehend it, almost spoils them for undertaking marriage without considerable emotional difficulty. This does not mean only meeting the inevitable complications of the first stages of living with someone else. But they have to learn that one can admit one's deepest emotions, need neither disown them nor wear them on the shoulder like chips; they have to come to the point of realising that there is nothing stuffy about trying to be a good husband and father, that one may be as much in the truth there as one will ever be in any area of life.[24]

So the 'political consciousness' which Hoggart seeks and which he strains to retrieve from a reconstructed 'old order' is that of the family – where one can 'admit one's deepest emotions' (acknowledge one's chips as feelings), and find as much 'truth' as one will ever find.

The 'scholarship boy' – the working-class boy in border country – is the point of connection between self and class, at which, in one sense, Leavisism can be mapped on to consciousness. Hoggart co-opts Leavisism for the working-class boy, but in doing so he carries with him a version of culture which contains none of the critique implied by Williams and Anderson's adherence to the term. Instead, he conflates culture with political consciousness, and believes, like Leavis, that if culture is radical enough it alone can constitute class-consciousness.[25] The test of cultural radicalism is whether it can produce or stand in for the supposed authenticity of the organic community. The difference between Hoggart and Leavis, however, is that Hoggart, though not a Marxist, nevertheless constructs his argument specifically with reference to the working class, and therefore gives at least the illusion of addressing a specifically working-class consciousness. The other difference is that Hoggart's use of the organic community centres more specifically than that of Leavis on the home and on the familial. Each of these distinctions has important implications – as we shall see – for socialism, and for girls, when educators draw on *The Uses of Literacy* for an educational practice.

Educators in the 1960s, as *New Left Review* bears out, come to education with a strong commitment to the view that education can produce consciousness, and specifically political consciousness. Education in the 1960s is at the centre of a rhetoric of revolutionary change.[26] Brian Jackson and Dennis Marsden's influential book, *Education and the Working Class* embraces the notion of 'the slow revolution being brought about by education', a notion which as we have seen received its initial charge from Raymond Williams – the long revolution – with its newly-inflected meaning from Juliet Mitchell's 'longest' revolution (which in a sense capped, or at least subsumed the idea of transformation through education with that of change instigated by women or withheld from them).[27] It is interesting, though, in theoretical terms and those of the Left argument, that studies of education and the working class tend to focus on the scholarship boy, and tend to be written by scholarship boys. In the first place, this ignores both girls and the secondary modern school where the majority of working-class children were. However powerful the critique of the grammar school that emerges from these studies is, there is a strong assumption that the grammar school *is* education, *is* the 'natural' home of culture and of the production of political consciousness. But in addition, this focusing on the working-class grammar-school boy highlights the individual and his aspiration to authentic and integrated selfhood via culture, rather than on the group – it privileges what we have identified as the 'bourgeois individualist' narrative of working-class consciousness, the autobiography, the moral realist account.[28] Perhaps in part because they carry this model with them themselves as scholarship boys, Jackson and Marsden also carry with them virtually intact that same model of 'culture' (sustaining and validating a sense of 'community') for which we have used the shorthand 'Leavisite'. In spite of the attempt to distance the version they want from 'middle-class values', they retain the crucial idea that culture *transmits* (self-evidently appropriate) values both across time (preserving what is authentic in the society) and *to* the individual. It is, apparently, as the individual intercepts the transmission of culture that he himself makes the transition from exclusion to inclusion, and *enabling* such access, to effect the transition, is the educator's goal for the working-class boy:

> On the one hand we have the central culture of our society ('the best that has been thought and known', 'the very culture of the feelings', 'that spontaneity which is the hardest of all') which must be preserved and transmitted; on the other hand we have institutions which do this for the middle class but not for the working-class majority. It seems to us that what we call our central culture and what the teachers call 'middle-class values' are by no means the same thing, and the problem is to disentangle one from the other in schools which are truly 'open'. When the head-teacher says 'I see grammar school education very strongly as a matter of communicating middle-class values to a "new" population', he is surely not saying something akin to Matthew Arnold's classic statement, but something contrary in spirit, provincial and partisan. It is worth quoting Arnold's statement in some fullness [there follows the complete 'sweetness and light' passage from Arnold's *Culture and Anarchy*].[29]

There is an evident confusion here about the relationship between 'values' and 'central culture': central culture apparently comes with its values ready built-in ('the best that has been thought and known', 'the very culture of the feelings', 'that spontaneity which is the hardest of all'), and these are *not* 'middle-class values', but something more universal – something suspiciously like 'ordinary values', which has here become something the scholarship boy ought to recognize as his.[30] In Jackson and Marsden's version, the focus is the scholarship boy's feelings: he *lives the experience of* the tension between the grammar school's assumption that the 'central culture' which it makes available unproblematically transmits 'ordinary values' (realized in the case of the middle-class boy), and his own awareness of difficulty in the encounter with values he can only perceive as middle-class, in the classroom. The individual scholarship boy faces the encounter with central culture alone, as a problem he must solve for himself – whether or not to embrace it, to endorse its values, and thereby make the transition out of anxiety and into the middle classes.

Effectively Jackson and Marsden present class as the problem, and culture as the solution. And quite unlike Williams, but quite like Hoggart, they thereby locate the tension – the sense of group otherness – necessary for class-consciousness within the feelings ('uprooted and anxious') of the scholarship boy, rather than in a characteristic response to culture itself ('an inequality of culture'). They want to redeem Arnold for democratic purposes, but they lose the sense of Arnold's place in a tradition which has many of those 'provincial and partisan' features above which they want to hold him – provincial and partisan in the sense of being historically localized to a set of arguments framed for and about Arnold's contemporary middle class and the centrality of its values, specifically in fear of class conflict.

The working-class children of Jackson and Marsden's study are characterized by their atypicality and their self-consciousness ('uprooted and anxious'). Like Hoggart's, theirs is the confusion of being the exception rather than the rule, the confusion of transition (the grammar school as transition for a minority *out of* the working class and *into* the middle class). The self-consciousness of being an exception meshes with the privileging of selfhood from and in the moral realist account, enabling self-consciousness to be passed off in the generalized conclusion as class-consciousness. And predictably, Jackson and Marsden propose the working-class mother, the 'organic' centre of the working-class family, as responsible for the specially receptive selfhood of the scholarship boy (as we have seen Orwell, and Thompson, and Hoggart do before):

behind the schooldays that we are now to examine, it is clear that the centres of power usually lay with the mother. In two thirds of the families there was either an equality of interest, or else the child could not or would not attest the major influence of one parent. In the 29 families where the child made distinctions about his parents' influence 23 claimed that the mother was the important and pressing parent, and six claimed this for the father. This could not altogether be accounted for by the mother's education or her superior station before the marriage, though both of these matter. Its roots seemed to push much deeper into the basic rhythms and expectations of working-class life, belonging to the whole pattern of social living in which the mother rather than the father was the organic centre.[31]

The mother is naturally identified with the 'basic rhythms and expectations of working-class [home] life', its 'organic centre'. As in Hoggart (after Leavis), the co-option of the family, and in particular the woman, to the 'organic' puts a particular emphasis on women to carry responsibility for a set of 'authentic' values (from an older order?) which will bridge from working class to middle class.[32]

What the autobiography of the scholarship boy produces for Jackson and Marsden when they come to their selection and interpretation of material for study is therefore *family* history in place of class history. We are reminded again of our Chapter 5 – the drive in latterday social and radical history away from confidence in class history, the pressure into an account of selfhood as a substitute for class-consciousness. In making their sample of eighty-eight working-class children, Jackson and Marsden are interestingly aware of the pull on them to answer questions about education and the working class via the family – 'It has been well-recognized that the answer to many of the questions we were raising would be found through a study of family life, and not of children in isolation.'[33]

Studies like those conducted by Jackson and Marsden, which map family history on to questions of the relationship between class inequality and education, depend crucially upon arguments tacitly taken over from Hoggart's *Uses of Literacy*. The Left account of education has continued to use Hoggart to tow it out from some of the problems of educational method and policy formation, encountered in the transition from grammar to comprehensive schooling. The comprehensive school, using Hoggart's model, would make culture available to all children without class-prejudice – the assumption of Arnold's 'central culture' *as* the source of equality in education is not apparently re-examined. What is lost from sight in these discussions (with the foregrounding of Hoggart, and the receding presence of Williams) is the acknowledgement (central to Williams's theoretical argument) that access alone will not suffice, that for the working-class child the encounter with culture itself is an *experience* of inequality ('Culture was the way in which the process of education, the experience of literature, and – for someone moving out of a working-class family to a higher education – inequality, came through').[34] Following that initiation, in which inequality is recognized in the encounter with culture, something must be done for working-class children as a group, to enable them to find their way through to their own class-consciousness:

> Labour educationalists have often shied away from the question of standards. The thinking behind comprehensive schooling, for example, did not really challenge the existing curriculum. Its main aim was to do away with restricted or privileged access. It therefore proposed a 'common school'. But it usually stopped at this institutional level, and failed to establish a curriculum which would create a 'common culture'. Sometimes, as in Harold Wilson's government during the 1960s, it was assumed that a grammar school curriculum could simply be democratized.[35]

That key question which Raymond Williams had addressed – how to engage with inequalities of culture as inequalities of class – carries over as the urgent and unresolved question in the treatment of the transition from grammar school to comprehensive school:

> It is a question of whether we can grasp the real nature of our society, or whether we persist in social and educational patterns based on a limited ruling class, a middle professional class, a large operative class, cemented by forces that cannot be challenged and will not be changed. The privileges and barriers, of an inherited kind, will in any case go down. It is only a question of whether we replace them by the free play of the market, or by a public education designed to express and create the values of an educated democracy and a common culture.[36]

Jackson and Marsden had taken the Arnoldian account of culture in an attempt to distance 'central culture' from 'middle-class values'. Hoggart attempted to assert the centrality of working-class values, against the grain of his Leavisism. But, as Raymond Williams sees, the problem of establishing a 'common culture' remains. In the early *New Left Review* conversation with Richard Hoggart, Raymond Williams puts that question:

> It's a question whether high culture is compatible with the ordinary values. What is the attitude, for example to a child going on with his education, when it's discovered that he's 'bright'? Is this considered odd, or is it regarded as a gift? . . . I've gone over this pretty carefully. With the girls, of course, it was different, though they'd go on to High School from the farms and the cottages, if they got scholarships; then some would drop out early, if they were wanted at home. But I can't think of any boys at the grammar school who dropped out like that.[37]

Hoggart's indirect answer to that question about 'high culture' and 'ordinary values' comes, we are arguing, in a particularly pervasive and influential form in *The Uses of Literacy*. Williams is here seeing that there is some problem of definition in relation to 'culture' and where it puts 'ordinary values'. (And it is worth noting that the problem registers itself, momentarily, in relation to girls too – but, as in Jackson and Marsden, without due attention.) In Hoggart, the formulation is taken up more simply as an assumption that the working-class boy is alienated from 'central culture' *because of* his 'ordinary values'. What *we* are arguing is that *The Uses of Literacy* does for education what Orwell and others do for the Left political account: via 'the family', it provides, for boys and men, a trans-class system of values ('ordinary values') which is the point at which the working-class boy and the middle-class boy constitute a unity in their relations to high or central culture. The compatability of high culture and ordinary values is thus engineered in some measure, via the familial, for them. But what this importantly leaves out for working-class boys is precisely that politicized work-place which was the point at issue between Hoggart and Williams in defining 'community', and ultimately class-consciousness.

In terms of our Chapter 5, the narrative of the working-class boy which is supposed to be his autobiography – a tale of 'ordinary values' – has placed him in education with a possibility of uniting with middle-class boys. But it is only in the transmuting of 'ordinary values' into conservatism – nostalgia for the organic community and traditional constructions of the family – that that union can take place. The working-class boy, alienated from a sense of his originating community as a place which might yield a politics of the work-place or an oppositional culture (out of accord with bourgeois individualism), has passed over to him an invitation to, and a means of sharing in, the conservatism of his middle-class contemporaries.

To the extent that Left education theory has vigorously embraced the culture model of equality in education, this conservatism has inadvertently come to stand in for the working-class boy's experience, in the name of working-class culture and class-consciousness. As a consequence, education has no real means of distinguishing between bourgeois individualism (or simply, individual self-interest), and a common interest or common culture shared through an individualized working-class consciousness. Ironically, we can see that conservatism for what it is when we are presented with 'working-class culture' in, say, Gareth Stedman Jones's analysis of nineteenth-century music-hall, but not when we hand it to working-class children as progressive schooling. In Chapter 5 we argue that models of 'working-class culture' in contemporary history draw us into an interpretation of the working-class as having lost its radicalism, its potential for political challenge. We discover here in education that we on the Left have built this conservatism into our account. In so far as the working-class boy and middle-class boy share values in education, it is in this common conservatism – presented to the working-class boy as both his 'experience' and as a possible model for an authentic selfhood.[38]

The parallel movement in history which we saw in Chapter 5 operating in relation to autobiography – male Left historians looking for authentic working-class experience and Left feminist historians looking into the unconscious – is also happening in education. Like working-class boys, girls are treated as if they were the bearers of conservatism. In the Left education account what happens is that 'culture' has two distinct sets of implications when taken into school-ing. Made available as a sounding-board for the individual child's 'lived experience', it produces self-consciousness for the working-class boy (anxiety about his class background, but a seeming unity in ordinary family values with his male peers of the middle class), and an 'unconscious' for girls (passive identification in the model, or a failure to identify anywhere at all as her peculiar personality problem).

In the 1970s and 1980s, there has been a considerable body of feminist writing about education which has focused on the anonymity of girls in the classroom. The journal *Screen Education* was an important forum for this debate. Judith Williamson's classic article, written for it, 'How does girl number twenty understand ideology?' gives us a powerful and shrewd insight into her own classroom. The lesson is about the representation of women in the media:

> My worst problem is Astrid. She looks, actually, very like the blonde heroines of the comic strips, her self image is clearly bound to the things we seem to be attacking. She sits at the front of the class and says literally nothing. She may file her nails, or just stare: I'm really worried about her. I offer to teach her with the other girls, but she doesn't particularly want to.[39]

Astrid says nothing. What are the theoretical options? She could identify with the boys in the class who have chosen the topic and are a majority view. But they tend to mock the images they see, and if she were to identify with that perspective she would be mocking herself. She does not share the boys' perspective because she is compromisingly within the account which the boys share. She does not line up with the girls either, because there is no particular group identity available to the girls, or if there is, it is only one which produces silence. Autobiography lends the boys their narrative; that account is not available to girls except in the object position – they are outside the consciousness to which the methodology of self-examination gives access, and are thereby produced as accessible only via psychoanalysis's exploration – its 'analysis' – of the 'unconscious'.

Nor is it enough to break the girls' silence with the talking cure. Therapy for girls squares neatly with the Hoggart model in giving girls the familial back to talk about, handing over responsibility again for 'ordinary values', without providing a group position which fuses the personal and cultural, from which to speak with the possibility of action, with agency. The need for therapy is *symptomatic* of the failure of a group identity (except in pathology) and of absence of political consciousness. It is not simply a question, for girls, of talking in class, but of finding a position, a shared identity, a common culture in Williams's terms, from which and in which to speak – a class in which to talk.

Where the problem had previously been viewed as that of the experience of culture as an experience of inequality carried over into schooling, the problem is now re-registered as one of adequate or inadequate selfhood. The exceptional working-class boy can locate a 'successful' selfhood in the conservatism (of family values) which unites him with the middle-class boy's individualism, but in the process he loses his common interest with other working-class boys. Analogously, an individual girl can line up with the boys if she is prepared to compete for individual distinction on those same individualistic terms. She too can find a unified selfhood in relation to family values, this time by treating them as part of the female symbolic, as internalized to her unconscious. The loss of common interest with other girls in the process is in this case more obvious, the loss of a group identity, of opposition, of the sense of class, in face of the call to construct an unfragmented self, an intact female psyche.

Anchored in the moral realist account, education offers 'treatment' as a substitute for instilling consciousness of group identity, recognition, interest. Any individual who appears, by virtue of his or her class position, to register 'culture' as an experience of inequality becomes a casualty, a 'case', an nonconforming selfhood, in need of a cure, to be nurtured and treated with sympathy. Guiltily, education offers therapy as its method – therapy as its most committed means of excavating class and cultural inequality (the boy in his comely life by the hearth; the girl in the Freudian unconscious where she dwells as organic mother). In both instances – for the boys and for the girls – the educational model drawn from our post-Hoggart scenario offers a 'treatment', a programme which strives to defuse any tensions which might accompany the reality of a sense of culture or class as a grounds for inequality. The psychoanalytic method, the therapy, does not even have to be explicitly conservative, only neutral, since the conservatism is already built into the model – in the autobiography handed to the working-class boy as his own, and in the unconscious handed to the girl in the form of the absence of a narrative of which she is the subject. Therapy becomes the unbiased strategy – at least a process, at least an activity, at least something to talk about, though never a means of alteration or change – to reaffirm the theoretical position that education has failed to provide answers to the problems of locating class-consciousness for the common interest, has failed to promote the long revolution.

Drawn right back to Raymond Williams's *Culture and Society*, we can see that that oppositional position available within 'culture' was intensely specific to that experience of 'moving out of a working-class home into an academic curriculum'. Williams's observations concerning the relationship between 'culture' and 'tradition' did indeed liberate our sense of relationships *inside* the tradition – a liberation which could operate effectively for individuals able to locate themselves in that particular tension between their personal history and an academic context, a tension which we have seen as characteristic of the 'scholarship boy'. For a while the Left account as initiated in the late 1950s and early 1960s saw that oppositional position *as* class-consciousness, and as the seed-bed of the long revolution. But that positing of an oppositional position *within* the tradition as class-consciousness sidestepped the issue of the fundamental and real inequality of the working-class individual of which the encounter with culture was simply, in a sense, a reminder (a symptom). Williams wanted 'to get the two experiences into relation', the working-class home that was his personal history into relation with the academic curriculum that was to be his life. Understanding the experience of inequality in relation to culture was to understand his own personal position, but – as he himself was the first to admit – was inadequate as a blueprint for a common culture in education, inadequate for those for whom that experience of successful transition was not even a possibility (graphically illustrated by his ackowledgement that it was plainly and simply 'different for the girls', experiencing transition only as a transition from the working-class home to the working-class home via education).

As we conclude this chapter, and begin to conclude this book, we are in a position to state bluntly that that slow revolution, that social and political change hoped for by Left educators in the 1950s and 1960s, has not been securely built into our theoretical or practical model of comprehensive schooling and other potentially open-access and democratic institutions and sectors of formal education. On the contrary, the potential for change, the potential to shape our society for a more equal future, is there only as an act of faith, as a shared commitment to the moral realist account of class, culture, experience, inequality, values. And as we conclude this chapter and this book and bring the argument full circle back to the Labour Party, we can begin to see that at the last general election the Labour Party simply did not have a sharp enough sense of crisis, of the urgent need to readdress the inequalities of culture and class which it is education's business to expunge.

Now, after the not-so-great debates of 1987 and 1988 over education, and the passing virtually unmodified of the Baker Bill after a remarkably long series of ineffectual consultation meetings with various groups from the electorate, we can see that it is all too easy to disable and dismantle the democratic tendencies of a Labour-inspired state education system. One of the most powerful thrusts of Conservative ideology has always been in the appeal to 'individualism', to selfhood, and to *choice*. Any political party, it is clear, has to take account of individuals in addressing the general interest. But what the Labour Party has shown itself signally unable to do is to *distinguish* its model of individuals working for the common interest, the general interest, from individuals as consumers engaged in competitive self-interest. If we should have learned anything from too many years of Conservative government, it is that a cultural and educational economy (as well as the obvious cash economy) of the market, taking the consumerist client as its starting point for the rights of the individual, is not just incompatible with any Left definition of the general interest, it is sharply hostile to it. Instead, all the pressures on the Labour Party seem to be to succumb to a notion of the individual as consumer, a selfhood collapsed into the operation of personal choice via cash and the credit card (and grouped with others on the basis of equivalent purchasing power and comparable credit ratings).

When we set out to write this book before the last general election in Britain, we saw this confusion and attempted to address it in our preface – the blurring of distinct ideologies which attach quite distinct meanings to 'individualism', the part that culture has played in confusing us about these distinctions. We see now, and particularly in addressing educational issues, that the maintaining of some such distinction is absolutely crucial to any conception of, or future for, socialism. To fail to make it is to leave the educational method and strategies we on the Left have devised far too open to appropriation, revealing that many of our methods were never much more than neutral, that their conception did not push through that crucial commitment to relieving the class inequalities of culture in education. It has been too easy for Left educational strategies to be taken over on behalf of a Conservative ideology which not only celebrates a selfhood defined in terms of the market economy, but glamourizes that conception as one central to democracy. This ideology – revealed explicitly in Kenneth Baker's education policy, and in the detail of the Baker Bill which is now on the statute book – is not one to which the Labour Party can succumb if it is to survive as the party of the oppressed, the party striving to redress inequality, if we are to survive as the Party which has anything to do with Bea Campbell's woman at the ironing board, or anything to do with defending what Raymond Williams and Edward Thompson have so compellingly theorized as the common interest.

Postscript
An exemplary life

I never had the privilege of being taught by him, but he was the most formative intellectual influence on my life. I often had the uncanny feeling that we had stumbled unawares on the same line of thinking – only he had given it, already, so lucid and compelling a formulation.[1]

Raymond Williams and I arrived in Cambridge simultaneously in 1961, he from a long stint in adult education to a college Fellowship, I from a year's teaching in a Northern secondary modern school to an undergraduate place. It was hard to say which of us was more alienated. Williams had made the long trek from a rural working-class community in Wales to a college which seemed to judge people (as I was to find out later to my cost) by how often they dined at High Table. He looked and spoke more like a countryman than a don, and had a warmth and simplicity of manner which contrasted sharply with the suave, off-hand style of the upper middle class establishment. He never got used to the casual malice of the Senior Combination Room, and was to write years later, in a fine obituary of F. R. Leavis, that Cambridge was 'one of the rudest places on earth . . . shot through with cold, nasty and bloody-minded talk'. I found myself marooned within a student body where everyone seemed to be well over six foot, brayed rather than spoke, stamped their feet in cinemas at the feeblest joke and addressed each other like public meetings in intimate cafes. It was a toss-up which of us was going to make it.[2]

There are even little instances of autobiographical encounter that can run into the sense of his work for me (that work, after all, is so full of a personal pressure): in the generation of Williams's father, my grandfather was also a farmworker's son and railway signalman. And then, like so many others, I have the closeness to the work, the knowledge of its importance. . . .

I have the impression of having gone over the same ground. 'A university degree in English didn't answer any of the questions that I found posed in the late 1940s.' In the late 1960s too, I could feel the same thing but the result of Williams at Cambridge . . . was at least that I had all the questions brought out and discussed; and what I then remember most, the education, was the central historical and theoretical problematization of all the basic concepts, literature and criticism for a start. For Williams, such concepts were always and quickly problems and not just analytic problems but those of 'historical movements that are still unresolved'.[3]

This postscript is written, as we indicated in our preface, by way of an acknowledgement of the impact the death of Raymond Williams had on the writing of this book. As we said there, it is an oblique kind of acknowledgement – not a further tribute to Williams (since the book was already in the process of exploring the long-term significance of his work, amongst other members of the New Left of the 1950s and 1960s), but a response to the quite rich body of material published in the weeks following Williams's entirely unexpected death. We felt that there were some distinctive features of these pieces of writing which we were coming to see as predictable, in the light of our own work on the long shadow cast by Williams across English Left thought, down to the 1980s.

In the tributes to Raymond Williams there was a real poignancy about the way in which Williams's colleagues and pupils wanted, apparently, to share his biography, to take on the personal history of 'the outstanding intellectual in British culture this century'.[4] It seemed to us that in a sense the staking of a claim to a shared personal history was also a staking of a claim to be the authentic intellectual successor – a claim that the similarity in the lived experience could be used to validate a shared intellectual approach also.

There is an obvious sense in which Williams's whole approach to culture invites this. Williams characterized his own search for an oppositional in relation to the 'tradition' and to culture as arising out of his own social origins. Speaking to Richard Hoggart, in 1960, we recall, he observed:

It's interesting, the way the books [*Culture and Society* and *The Uses of Literacy*] were built. I can remember my own first impulse, back at the end of the 'forties. I felt isolated, except for my family and my immediate work. The Labour Government had gone deeply wrong, and the other tradition that mattered, the cultural criticism of our kind of society, had moved, with Eliot, right away from anything I could feel. It seemed to me I had to try to go back over the tradition, to look at it again and get it into relation with my own experience, to see the way the intellectual tradition stood in the pattern of my own growing-up. As I saw the cultural tradition then, it was mainly Coleridge, Arnold, Leavis and the Marxists, and the development, really, was a discovery of relationships inside the tradition, and also a discovery of other relationships: Cobbett and Morris, for example, who brought in parts of my experience that had been separate before. Getting the tradition right was getting myself right, and that meant changing both myself and the usual version of the tradition. I think this is one of the problems we're both conscious of: moving out of a working-class home into an academic curriculum, absorbing it first and then, later, trying to get the two experiences into relation.[5]

'I think this is one of the problems we're both conscious of: moving out of a working-class home into an academic curriculum, absorbing it first and then, later, trying to get the two experiences into relation' – that is the same positioning the writers of the tributes adopt, that 'trying to get the two experiences into relation'. But what Williams is moving towards here, as we showed in Chapter 6, is a way of accounting for his growing theoretical understanding that class-consciousness can be constructed as a set of relations to culture, and his belief that Hoggart's rather different theoretical position nevertheless takes its origin from a similar encounter, as a working-class boy, with high culture in the grammar school.

So there is a kind of *solidarity* to be derived from those common roots, those common problems with getting different kinds of experience into relation. The question is, how far does such solidarity take us (or rather, them)? And the answer, it seems to us, must lie very close to our explorations of Chapters 4 and 5, where we found that 'personal history' came, in the New Left account, to stand in increasingly *for* class-consciousness, and for the 'shared values' which Williams maintained were the neccesary underpinning for a working-class movement forwarding 'the long revolution'.

What Raymond Williams contributed to English Left thought was a profoundly original and lastingly influential theory of the relationship between class-consciousness and culture. We have argued throughout the present book that Williams's contributions shaped Left debate in the 1960s in such a way that it is necessary to unravel that influence with care, if we are to take the debate further – if we are to continue that debate appropriately through the 1980s and into the 1990s. We have argued that that very late-nineteenth-century culture, which Williams identified as such a potentially positive (oppositional) source of values for a specifically working-class consciousness, confines women to the domestic, the family – uses women to *give* value to the working man, via the family and the home. Unless we recognize and respond to this, we have argued, we will not be able to retrieve women as social and political agents, and to incorporate them into an account of contemporary class-consciousness.

Yet the obituary notices are not about Williams's theory, they are about his *example*, his exemplary life. According to those notices, he exemplified his own version of consciousness of inequality, as inequality of culture – class-consciousness *as* a particular sense of his own encounter with culture in education:

> Culture was the way in which the process of education, the experience of literature, and – for someone moving out of a working-class family to a higher education – inequality, came through. What other people, in different situations, might experience more directly as economic or political inequality, was naturally experienced, from my own route, as primarily an inequality of culture: an inequality which was also, in an obvious sense, an uncommunity.[6]

The writers of the testimonies to Raymond Williams's achievement align themselves very precisely with this experience – someone moving out of a working-class family to a higher education, and an accompanying intense *sense* of inequality.[7] Marginality within institutional academic life is represented again and again in these pieces as a matter of *autobiography*, a feeling, a state of mind. But Williams is talking about a politics, about being politicized. He is talking about the way in which he was *able* to politicize his study of culture because of the recognition that it was there that he could articulate his sense of inequality – that his class-consciousness could be articulated there. He is talking about the way in which his own experience could be articulated as that of a member of a particular class and community, the *shared* quality of which – via culture – made it politically valuable.

What is striking about the tribute-writers' use of the supposedly shared sense of inequality of culture, by contrast, is the way in which it privileges the individual, and *erases* the crucial political distinctions. Derek Robbins, replying to the passage by Heath which heads this Postscript, noted that 'there must surely be something wrong about Heath's acknowledgement that in the late 1960s he could "feel the same thing" as Williams had in the late 1940s'.[8] 'What other people, in different situations, might experience more directly as economic or political inequality, was naturally experienced, from my own route, as primarily an inequality of culture: an inequality which was also, in an obvious sense, an uncommunity'; this is the experience Heath says he shared with Williams. But, as Robbins points out, Williams's encounter with culture must, on the strength of his own theory of the connections between culture and particular communities, have been *distinct* from Heath's twenty years later, however much it may be said at the personal, individualized level, to have *felt* the same. In a remarkably similar move, Eagleton's 'It was hard to say which of us was more alienated' collapses politics and consciousness (the different material conditions, the different institutional positions) into how being at Cambridge *felt* ('He never got used to . . .', 'I found myself marooned').

Stuart Hall does not claim to share a railway-signalman relative, or a British working-class home with Williams. Rather, he 'often had the uncanny feeling that [they] had stumbled unawares on the same line of thinking' – that is his sense of sharing a heritage with Williams. E. P. Thompson remembers Williams as 'an intensely political man'.[9] Here, surely, is a stronger thread to follow, to recapture the 'exemplary' in Williams. The political thought, and the political activism, as providing some kind of bearings for the development of further thought and further activism, in the decades to come. And both voiced, not in the name of an individual, but of that *community* – those commonly held values which serve to define a group as socially distinct – in which women and men move together towards a more equal future.

Notes

Preface

1 This earlier version was written for what was originally intended as a *Festschrift* for Raymond Williams, edited by Terry Eagleton (Cambridge: Polity, 1989), 'Homage to Orwell; the dream of a common culture and other minefields', 108–29.
2 Judith Williamson, *Decoding Advertisements: Ideology and Meaning in Advertising* (London: Marion Boyars, 1978).
3 So the recurrent debate on the Left about how to 'use' television admits of only one answer: television is a medium for communication as well as for marketing. The Tories have the monopoly of the latter; how about trying the former (policies not slogans)?
4 Bea Campbell, *Wigan Pier Revisited: Poverty and Politics in the 80s* (London: Virago, 1984), 113–14.
5 After the success of the red roses during the campaign, it is troubling now to realize how poignantly all those blood-red bouquets represented the exclusion of armies of working women from those on the platform receiving them.
6 We owe this insight in part to Joan Scott, 'History and difference', *Daedelus* 116 (1987), 93–118.

1 Homage to Orwell

1 Raymond Williams, 'Orwell', *Politics and Letters: Interviews with New Left Review* (London: Verso, 1979), 384.
2 Bea Campbell, *Wigan Pier Revisited: Poverty and Politics in the 80s* (London: Virago, 1984), 5.
3 ibid.
4 ibid., 217.
5 Gareth Stedman Jones, *Marxism Today*, July 1984, 39.
6 ibid.
7 ibid., 38. That 'full sense of a way of life' which Stedman Jones quotes from Williams lies at the root of the problem. As a version of 'society'

it belongs firmly to the cultural sphere, where, as we shall show, it both invokes the private and domestic, but then for historical reasons excludes women as subjects.

8   ibid., 39.

9   ibid., 40.

10   There is an interesting lesson to be learned, actually, from the dust-jackets of consecutive printings of the Penguin text (we happen to have three in front of us, identically paginated and differing only in their covers). The 1962 cover shows a crowd of working men and a pit head in a kind of photo montage, and is labelled 'literature' (implicitly); the 1974 cover is a line drawing of Orwell in a cloth cap, with the pit head in the background, and is labelled 'autobiography'; the 1986 cover is a 'designer' graphic of miners in the pit cage, coloured in pastels, and is labelled 'social history'.

11   See for instance, in our own work, L. Jardine, '"Girl talk" (for boys on the left), or marginalising feminist critical praxis', *Oxford Literary Review* 8 (1986), 208–17; J. Swindells, 'Liberating the subject?' A reading of the *Diaries of Hannah Cullwick*, in The Personal Narrative's Group (ed.), *Interpreting Women's Lives* (Indiana University Press, 1989).

12   Thompson explicitly relates *William Morris* and Williams's *Culture and Society* in the 'Postscript' to the revised 1976 edition: 'The typing of this Romantic critique as "regressive", "utopian", and "idealist" is a facile way of getting out of the problem, for an alternative way of reading that tradition had been proposed, not only in my book, in 1955, but, very cogently, by Raymond Williams in *Culture and Society* in 1958' ('Romanticism, moralism and utopianism: the case of William Morris', *New Left Review* 99 (1976), 83–111, 90).

13   Williams himself draws attention to this 'moment' in *Politics and Letters* – particularly to the close connection between his first two books and Thompson's *The Making of the English Working Class*, published in 1963, but under way in the late 1950s.

14   'The generalization of this use of the term [culture] characterized the Left in the fifties, and was responsible for some important insights into British society: this was the moment of Richard Hoggart's *Uses of Literacy*' (Perry Anderson, 'Components of the national culture', *New Left Review* 50 (1968), 3–57, 5).

15   As per the text, but this is surely an elision; on page 5 Anderson has specified that the 'one serious work of socialist theory' is *Culture and Society*. See also a relevant footnote in an earlier piece by Anderson: 'It is immensely significant, incidentally, that the only major theoretical departure in English social thought in the last decade – *The Long Revolution* – has derived from a writer trained in literary criticism. This was perhaps the only source from which it could have come, since the literary tradition of *Culture and Society* was the British substitute for classical sociology or a philosophical socialism in the 19th century' ('Socialism and pseudo-empiricism', *New Left Review* 35 (1966), 2–42, 23). Both Anderson and Thompson have a tendency to run the two works together, which is, we are arguing, not at all unexpected.

16 ibid., 55–6.
17 Anderson, 'Socialism and pseudo-empiricism', 36–7.
18 ibid., 37.
19 Williams, *Politics and Letters*, 97–8.
20 We tend to think that he was further read by a younger generation of Left critics as *exposing* the historical reality of class conflict *through* apparently bourgeois texts (traditionally beyond the pale for the radical critic). So, when Williams is discussing 'culture', they are discussing canonical authors; and when Williams subjects 'culture' to analysis, they are wrapped up in the nineteenth-century novel – source for them of genuine 'narrative', to be deconstructed for its social relations and cultural practices.
21 Williams himself has always been particularly upset when class has got left out in versions of his work, and his 'long revolution' has been reduced to cultural evolution. See, for example, T. Eagleton and B. Wicker (eds), *From Culture to Revolution* (London: Sheed & Ward, 1968), 296–7. Historically this is an interestingly symptomatic volume for the *fortuna* of Williams's work. It post-dates *The Long Revolution*, and is contemporary with a period of significant student dissent, yet in its treatment of 'culture' it focuses on *Culture and Society*, and English studies to the virtual exclusion of history.
22 See p. 8.
23 Williams, *Politics and Letters*, 112.
24 It is worth noting how women habitually get invoked when there is a panic about class (see also Williams's remark about Virginia Woolf above). Mr Eliot's class might problematize the discussion, without an elderly gentlewoman to take responsibility for his Tradition.
25 *New Left Review* 9 (1961), 24–33, 24–5.
26 ibid., 25.
27 Such is Thompson's emphasis that we at first took his remarks to allude to Williams's own *position* in a major university. It was Raymond Williams himself, reading an early draft of this chapter, who pointed out to us that at this time he was in fact an adult education lecturer (personal communication, 1987). For yet another account of the circumstances of this crucial review see Thompson, 'The politics of theory', in R. Samuel (ed.), *People's History and Socialist Theory* (London: Routledge & Kegan Paul, 1981), 396–408, 397–8.
28 *New Reasoner* 9 (1959), 74–83, 78.
29 ibid., 80–1.
30 'Orwell', 52.
31 In *Exiles and Emigrés*, Eagleton finds himself making this problem explicit in relation to what he calls 'the lower middle-class novel' (which Orwell supposedly writes): 'Orwell himself, of course, was not lower middle class in origin: he was born into an equally insecure stratum at the lower end of the upper class, but transplanted those tensions into what emerges, in some of his novels, as a definitively lower middle-class ethos'. Hmmm! (*Exiles and Emigrés: Studies in Modern Literature* (London: Chatto & Windus, 1970), 73).

32 'Trained at Eton to be a snob but disgusted by the oppressive methods he had applied in the Burma police, George Orwell set out as deliberately as William Cobbett to make contact with the working class in England. These "Urban Rides" of his, whether to Wigan or Sheffield, supply us with a series of factual, shocking, but sublimely human reports on the state of the nation in a time of mass unemployment' (London: Penguin, 1937 dustjacket). 'Commissioned by the Left Book Club, George Orwell set out to write the urban equivalent of Cobbett's *Rural Rides* and describe the great industrial wastelands of Yorkshire and Lancashire' (London: Penguin, 1986 dustjacket).

33 E. P. Thompson, *The Making of the English Working Class* (London: Gollancz, 1963; Penguin edn, 1968), 820.

34 Williams, *Politics and Letters*, 385–6.

35 Orwell, *Road to Wigan Pier*, 21.

36 For a full account of this tendency in Orwell's text see Daphne Patai, *The Orwell Mystique: A Study in Male Ideology* (Amherst: University of Massachusetts Press, 1984).

37 We are grateful to Dorothy Armstrong for making this point to us.

38 Orwell, *Road to Wigan Pier*, 29.

39 ibid., 31.

40 See in particular, Patai, *Orwell Mystique*.

41 Campbell, *Wigan Pier Revisited*, 98.

42 ibid., 99.

43 Orwell, *Road to Wigan Pier*, 104–5.

44 See J. Swindells, *Victorian Writing and Working Women* (Cambridge: Polity, 1985), *passim*.

45 Campbell, *Wigan Pier Revisited*, 57–9.

46 We would in fact argue that Campbell is misled by 'masculinity' into representing the problem as one of *sexuality*, and involving Arthur Munby and muscular pit-girls to invalidate Orwell's account.

47 S. Orwell and I. Angus, *The Collected Essays, Journalism and Letters of George Orwell*, vol. 1, *An Age Like This 1920–1940* (London: Penguin, 1970), 210–13, 234–6, 237–40.

48 ibid., *Diary*, 239–40.

49 ibid., 236.

50 ibid., 202–4.

51 Orwell, *Road to Wigan Pier*, 11.

52 ibid., 6–7.

53 Campbell, *Wigan Pier Revisited*, 5.

54 Judith Williamson has drawn attention to this 'superior' stance of the critic. See particularly, 'How does girl number twenty understand ideology?', *Screen Education* 40 (1981–2), 80–7.

55 For a particularly clear account of the historically developing theories of relations between 'dominant' and 'popular' culture, see M. Shiach, *Theories of Popular Culture* (Cambridge: Polity, in press).

56 T. Eagleton, 'Mutations of critical ideology', *Criticism and Ideology* (London: New Left Books, 1976), 11–43.

57 *New Left Review* 95 (1976), 3–23.

58 Anthony Barnett, 'Raymond Williams and Marxism: a rejoinder to Terry Eagleton', *New Left Review* 99 (1976), 47–64, 48.

59 Eagleton did so in terms which damagingly severed Williams's critical thought from his politics, to produce an unjustly harsh judgement – provoking immediate indignantly defensive replies from Anthony Barnett and E. P. Thompson: Barnett, op. cit.; E. P. Thompson, 'Romanticism, moralism and utopianism: the case of William Morris', *New Left Review* 99 (1976), 83–111 ('Afternote', 110–11).

60 Eagleton, 'Criticism and politics', 10.

61 Raymond Williams, 'Culture and revolution: a comment', in T. Eagleton and B. Wicker (eds), *From Culture to Revolution* (London: Sheed & Ward, 1968), 22–34, 22.

62 Raymond Williams, *Culture and Society 1780–1950* (London: Chatto & Windus, 1959; Penguin edn, 1961), 248–9.

63 See most fully Francis Mulhern, *The Moment of Scrutiny* (London: New Left Books, 1979).

64 Eagleton, 'Criticism and politics', 23.

65 Thompson, 'Romanticism, moralism and utopianism: the case of William Morris', 111.

66 It did not help, of course, that Eagleton himself made overly grand claims for the 'difficulties' he had detected in Williams's work.

67 Williams, *Politics and Letters*, 149.

68 Campbell, *Wigan Pier Revisited*, 113–4.

2 'In a Voice Choking with Anger'

1 E. P. Thompson, *The Making of the English Working Class* (London: Gollancz, 1963; Penguin edn, 1968), 939.

2 There is an attempt at linking 'culture' and 'history' in Richard Johnson (ed.), *Working Class Culture* (London: Hutchinson, 1979).

3 Juliet Mitchell, *Women: The Longest Revolution* (London: Virago, 1984), 17–18.

4 There is a good representative example of this absence of place in *New Left Review* 24 (1964), in the 'Scanner' section, in which, according to the editorial in the same issue, editorial opinion is recorded, without being ascribed to an individual author ('As well as the articles signed by members of the Editorial Committee, the opinion and point of view of *NLR* will be found in many of the comments in the "Scanner"' (4)). There, under the title 'The regiments of women', Mitchell (presumably – the only female member of the editorial board) discusses the problem that women fail to vote Labour (a favourite 'bad faith' topic then as now for women on the Left), and urges the Left to campaign to bring women into the Labour movement: 'In every election since the war there has been a yawning disparity between men and women voters for the Labour Party. So much so that had women voted for the Labour Party in equal numbers with men *there would have been a Labour Government in power uninterruptedly since 1945*. Even today the percentage difference in support for the Labour Party is striking: an 18.5 per cent lead over

the Conservatives among men, but one of only 4 per cent among women' (65). This intervention occasions *absolute silence* in that issue of *NLR* and thereafter, whereas comparable interventions about men and the Labour Movement customarily provoke response and debate.

5 *Politics and Letters: Interviews with New Left Review* (London: Verso, 1979), 148.

6 It is striking to us that in all the retrospective literature which we shall have occasion to refer to, reflecting upon the political significance of the arguments between the old and new New Left, Juliet Mitchell is not once mentioned. Yet she was a member of the editorial board from the beginning of its 'revision' under Perry Anderson (1962).

7 Mitchell, *Women*.

8 1962 was also the year in which Mitchell became a member of the 'New' editorial board of *NLR*. So Williams and the transition in *NLR* editorship – a transition, as we shall see, fraught with ideological difficulty – provide a context for Mitchell's crucial work.

9 *NLR* 41, 78.

10 ibid., 79.

11 See Jane Gallop, 'Juliet Mitchell and the "human" sciences', in T. Brennan (ed.), *Between Feminism and Psychoanalysis* (London: Routledge, 1989), who 'reads' history deconstructively as the problematic Mitchell term, without understanding *its* history.

12 Hoare's response to Mitchell might be compared with Anthony Barnett's response to Terry Eagleton in the same journal, when Eagleton offered a critique of Raymond Williams, and the board chose in the end not to offend Williams. In both cases, we feel, a response at length in the pages of the journal from a member of the editorial board constitutes an official policy statement on the topic, on the part of *New Left Review*, strategically made *outside* the journal's own editorial.

13 Mitchell, *Women*.

14 *The Poverty of Theory* (London: Merlin, 1978), 35. This account of Perry Anderson's takeover of *NLR* makes a striking contrast with Thompson's later account, in 'An open letter to Leszek Kolakowski' (1973), reprinted in *The Poverty of Theory*, 92–192: 'Our unresolved intellectual debates [of the Old intellectual Left] remained unresolved. . . . And for the irresolute, 'history' has little patience. We reached a point of personal, financial and organizational exhaustion; and at this moment, the agent of history appeared, in the form of Perry Anderson. We were exhausted: he was intellectually fertile, immensely self-concentrated, decisive. We saw, in a partnership with him and his colleagues, an opportunity to regenerate the review and to recuperate our own squandered intellectual resources. We did not, as it happens, anticipate that the first expression of his decisiveness would be to dismiss the review's founders from its board. We were, it turned out, insufficiently "rigorous": which was true. We were confined within a narrow nationalistic culture and unaware of the truly internationalist Marxist discourse. . . . And we were not intellectually "reputable": which meant that our work was not well-regarded in Oxford. . . . I explain all this

because I find even now (outside of Britain) some confusion as to the intellectual relationship between the first and the second *New Left Review*. Since taking editorial control in 1963 Perry Anderson and his colleagues have conducted the review with system, conviction and decision. There was, however, a fracture in the passage from one tradition to another, which was never exposed to principled discussion. It was a very English transition: that is (according to one's viewpoint) gentlemanly and tolerant, or otiose and manipulative. It was not until 1965 that I raised, in the pages of [*Socialist*] *Register*, objections to certain interpretations in the (mutated) *New Left Review*: these pointed to ulterior questions of some significance, although I was inhibited both by my own sense of the shared fellowship of the Left and by editorial advice, from pressing every objection home. In due course, and perhaps with less sense of either inhibition, Anderson replied. His reply, in my view, neither answered my objections nor opened up new problems of significance. That is where matters remain' (101–2). We shall later consider Anderson's own version of these events.

15 P. Anderson, 'Socialism and pseudo-empiricism', *NLR* 35 (1966), 2.
16 For example, Thompson's name does not figure anywhere in the main title of Perry Anderson's *Arguments Within English Marxism* (London: New Left Books and Verso, 1980), although the book is a closely worked critique, item by item, of Thompson's published work. And Anderson and Thompson tend to acknowledge one another's influence indirectly and elliptically in their prefaces.
17 'Everything *NLR* had stood for' naturally entirely ignores Mitchell and women's issues, but perhaps we are labouring the point.
18 Anderson, 'Socialism and pseudo-empiricism', 6.
19 See pp. 21–2.
20 'Romanticism, moralism, utopianism: the case of William Morris', *NLR* 99 (1976), 83–111, 110.
21 But, as we shall show in the next chapter, Thompson's 'Postscript' does mark his explicit adopting of *Williams* as an intellectual ally.
22 Perry Anderson, *Arguments Within English Marxism*, 1–2.
23 The title omits all mention of Thompson. However, the classification data alongside the ISBN number specifies 'Anderson, Perry / Arguments Within English Marxism. / 1. Thompson, Edward Palmer'.
24 Eagleton, *Criticism and Ideology* (London: New Left Books, 1976), 43, for 'scientific knowledge'.
25 Williams, *Politics and Letters*, 108.
26 ibid., 77.
27 ibid., 66.
28 In *Politics and Letters* (67) Williams claims that his contact with Leavisism was 'secondhand' – derived from Mankowitz and Collins. What is most significant about this is probably the need Williams feels to sustain a kind of historical distance from Leavis – he at least never sat at Leavis's feet. He goes to the trouble of establishing this distance more explicitly by citing a specific occasion on which Leavis 'leaning against the wall at the back of the room', during a paper delivered by

L. C. Knights, nodded 'approvingly' when Mankowitz publicly disagreed with Williams (his close friend) during the questioning.

29 Francis Mulhern, *The Moment of 'Scrutiny'* (London: New Left Books, 1979).

30 Williams, *Politics and Letters*, 67–8.

31 This was, of course, what Eagleton tried to point out in that infamous *New Left Review* article.

32 We should compare this with *Scrutiny*-style history as discussed by Mulhern, op. cit., 75.

33 Thompson, *Poverty of Theory*, 194.

34 ibid., 197.

35 Thompson, 'The Long Revolution I', *NLR*, 1961, 24–33, 26.

36 ibid., 26.

37 ibid., 33.

38 It is striking how little of the two-part review is about *The Long Revolution* at all.

39 R. Williams, *The Long Revolution* (London: Chatto & Windus, 1961), 122.

40 Thompson, 'The Long Revolution I', 31.

41 ibid., 32.

42 ibid.

43 ibid., 38.

44 Williams, *Politics and Letters*, 133–4.

45 When one of the present authors received a prominent hostile review to her book in 1984, Raymond Williams recalled again to her the overwhelmingly discouraging and hostile reviews *The Long Revolution* had received, at the very moment when he was appointed a Lecturer at Cambridge, and the distress that caused him.

46 In view of the enormity of this suggestion, perhaps we should be specific. There is not a single mention of *The Making of the English Working Class*, nor indeed of Thompson, in 'Origins of the present crisis'. In Tom Nairn's continuation of that debate in 'The nature of the Labour Party 1 and 2', (*NLR* 27 (1964), 38–65; *NLR* 28, 33–62), there is a single reference to Thompson, with the enigmatic footnote 'op. cit.', although *The Making of the English Working Class* is nowhere cited. However, this does alert us to the fact that Nairn *had* reviewed *The Making of the English Working Class*, some issues previously, in an article entitled 'The English working class', billed in the editorial as a continuation of the 'large-scale historical analysis begun in our last number by Perry Anderson's article on "The origins of the present crisis"' (*NLR* 24 (1964), 4). This review is singularly lacking in any insight into the *theoretical* significance of Thompson's book, although Anderson claims that it confirms that *New Left Review* was taking Thompson seriously at this date (*Arguments Within English Marxism*, 132). Anderson also makes a rather laboured point of saying that the *New Left Review* editorial board already had *The Making of the English Working Class* (in proof?) in 1962 ('Who can criticize [the old *New Left Review* board], when among other things they gave us *The Making of the*

English Working Class, which was published the next year?' (137)). Our considered view is that Nairn had read it and Anderson hadn't, and that since Nairn failed entirely to recognize its theoretical importance, it was deemed irrelevant to 'Origins of the present crisis'.

47 Anderson, 'Origins of the present crisis'.
48 Turning to the history again. Since Anderson and Thompson were already embroiled in disagreement over the editorial policy of *New Left Review*, it is hardly surprising that Anderson should have overlooked one of the 'Old Guard' (Thompson was 35) as simply not relevant to the 'sophisticated', 'international' theoretical framework within which 'Origins' was being written. The 'internationalism' of *New Left Review*'s later policy is deliberately opposed to Thompson-style (Old Guard) English nationalism (see, for instance, 'Internationalism' in *Arguments Within English Marxism*).
49 Anderson, 'Origins of the present crisis', 27.
50 ibid., 49.
51 Given how closely Anderson and Nairn worked together, we can in fact infer from Nairn's articles that they *had* read *The Making of the English Working Class* in 1964, but judged it largely irrelevant. See once again the hilarious reference to 'Thompson op. cit.' (*not* in fact cit.) in 'Anatomy 2'. Nairn tends to be explicit where Anderson discreetly hints.
52 'Origins of the present crisis', 45. His observations are of course retrospectively revealing: rather the non-labouring gentleman amateur and member of the SDP than a member of the *working* class.
53 However, it is *not* Anderson's 'Anglo-phobia' which leads Thompson's championing of the working classes towards English culture, as Richard Johnson suggests: 'One further consequence of the approach via failure is worth mentioning in passing. It seriously skewed the Thompson response. On most but not all historical questions, the ones Edward Thompson knows most about, he is much more accurate than Anderson. But Anderson's Anglo-phobia set off a great spiral of cultural chauvinism so that a good part of the argument became the richness or otherwise of English bourgeois culture rather than its tendencies and effect. 'The peculiarities of the English' remains a fascinating essay and a formidable polemic but is not always addressed to the most important issues' (Richard Johnson, *The Peculiarities of the English Route: Barrington Moore, Perry Anderson and English Social Development*, Stencilled Occasional Papers 26 (Birmingham: University of Birmingham, Centre for Contemporary Cultural Studies, 1975? (n.d.)), 19). Thompson's interest in 'the richness or otherwise of English bourgeois culture' is, we are arguing, absolutely crucial.
54 Anderson, *Arguments Within English Marxism*, 29–30.
55 ibid., 147. Contrast Anderson's clear account of the importance of Williams's notion of culture for Left thought which we quote in Chapter 1.
56 Anderson, 'Origins of the present crisis', 27.
57 Anderson, introduction to *Arguments Within English Marxism*.
58 Thompson, *Making of the English Working Class*, 8–9.

59 ibid., 10; cit. Anderson, *Arguments Within English Marxism*, 30.
60 E. P. Thompson, 'Romanticism, moralism and utopianism: the case of Willliam Morris', *New Left Review* 99 (1976), 83–111, 109.
61 ibid., 109.
62 See p. 1.

3 Writing History with a Vengeance

1 *NLR* 41 (1967), 79–81.
2 *NLR* 41 (1967), 83.
3 Robbie Gray, 'The Victorian visionary', *Marxism Today*, March 1984, 30–3, 30.
4 E. P. Thompson, *William Morris: Romantic to Revolutionary* (London: Merlin, 1955), 717.
5 The *Marxism Today* article actually uses the phrase 'the making of socialism' as a version of Morris's Marxism.
6 Sea-cadet P. Anderson, *Arguments Within English Marxism* (London: New Left Books and Verso, 1980), 158.
7 In spite of Lindsay's own Marxism. More later.
8 E. P. Thompson, *William Morris*, 'Postscript: 1976', 763–810.
9 ibid.
10 ibid., 802.
11 Witness all those National Portrait Gallery postcards of William Morris on all those undergraduate socialist mantlepieces.
12 Just as *The Long Revolution* was published just *before* Thompson's *The Making of the English Working Class*, and Williams, in the *Politics and Letters* interviews expresses regret that the explicative force of the latter was not therefore brought to bear (*Politics and Letters: Interviews with New Left Review* (London: Verso, 1979)).
13 Thompson, 'Postscript', 809.
14 Thompson *always* acknowledges and covertly answers criticism of his own writing.
15 Thompson, 'Postscript', 785. On the same page, it is from Romanticism that 'moral realism' comes.
16 ibid., 775–6.
17 Williams, *Politics and Letters*, 109.
18 ibid., 115.
19 ibid., 112.
20 Thompson, 'Postscript', 779.
21 Raymond Williams, *Culture and Society 1780–1950* (London: Chatto & Windus, 1959; Penguin edn, 1961), 144–5.
22 ibid., 159.
23 ibid., 145.
24 ibid.
25 G. Lukács, *The Meaning of Contemporary Realism* (London: Merlin, 1963).
26 We recognize that the topic is a large one, but we are also convinced that the fact that a meal has been made out of it by some ought not

to allow it to dominate a discussion which is trying to get to more substantial issues.

27 For Williams on aestheticism see *Culture and Society*, 142.

28 J. Lindsay, *William Morris* (London: Constable & Co., 1975), 348.

29 Raymond Williams, *Problems in Materialism and Culture* (London: Verso and New Left Books, London, 1980), 204.

30 But see Williams, *Culture and Society*, 159: 'I would willingly lose *The Dream of John Ball* . . . and even *News from Nowhere* – in . . . which the weaknesses of Morris's general poetry are active and disabling.'

31 *News from Nowhere*, 193–7.

32 Perry Anderson, noting (with embarrassment?) the women's serving role in the text (maybe Mitchell pointed it out), hurriedly adds: 'In fact, the discrimination of women is less than it might seem at first sight, since men too are predominantly assigned manual roles in a world which celebrates an essentially similar dexterity in homes, on the roads or in the fields' (*Arguments Within English Marxism*, 167).

33 Our first reaction when we saw the red rose as the new logo of the Labour Party was a reaction to the place of women in this history – 'Oh no, not red roses'. That we were persuaded to the image during the election campaign is, we think, a testament to the power which works within us all as that history of English culture.

34 E. P. Thompson, *William Morris*, 75–6.

35 The first two appearances of Jane Burden are both descriptions of her (aesthetic) appearance.

36 On the priority of family values in novel narratives (the literary version of history) see Tony Tanner, *Adultery and the Novel* (Baltimore: Johns Hopkins University Press, 1979).

37 Thompson, *William Morris*, 48. This is the first introduction of Jane. The second is even more telling, but difficult to excerpt: Thompson follows the observation, 'But these years were to bring their lasting influence in yet another form – in Morris's choice of the beautiful Jane Burden as his wife' (64) with a long digressionary account of Pre-Raphaelite attitudes to women, which takes the form of quotation of passages describing female beauty ('She was slim and thin . . . a little above the middle height of women, well-knit and with a certain massiveness about her figure' (65); 'My lady seems of ivory / Forehead, straight nose, and cheeks that be / Hollow'd a little mournfully' (66)) from Morris's *literary* works, and returns finally to that marriage with the observation, 'How far the most famous Pre-Raphaelite models – and in particular 'Lizzie' Siddal and Jane Burden – were cast by temperament and nature for their role, and how far they were created anew in the image of the ideal it is impossible to judge' (74). The literary and the 'history' are by now inextricably entwined – so much so that all these pages appear in the index under 'Jane Morris (Mrs William Morris)', poetry and all (indeed, following up the indexed allusions to Jane is a revelation – she is indexed on numbers of pages where her name *never appears*, but where William's representation of love un-requited, passion unfulfilled, does).

38 It is quite disturbing how widely one can replicate those descriptions of Jane (in Morris and in Thompson) in other literature of the period, from Wilkie Collins to Thomas Hardy.

39 Lindsay, *William Morris*, 154.

40 The James passage also includes a 'literary' description of William Morris's appearance; Thompson gives neither space nor attention to this – he knows *pictures* of William Morris are not part of his-story.

41 Anderson, *Arguments Within English Marxism*, 158. We find it striking that it should be *William Morris* which Thompson felt called for a substantial legitimizing addition, rather than *The Making of the English Working Class*.

42 Anderson, *Arguments Within English Marxism*, 167. Actually Anderson betrays some unease, in his recognition of the demeaning role medievalism gives to women, and then his lame acceptance of it on the grounds that it may be less discriminatory than it at first appears.

43 Thompson, *Making of the English Working Class*, 12.

44 Thompson, *William Morris*, 74–5.

45 Lindsay, *William Morris*, 92.

46 ibid., 102.

47 Thompson, *William Morris*, 158–60, 167.

4 Talking her Way Out of It

1 Juliet Mitchell, *Women: The Longest Revolution* (London: Virago, 1984), 19–20.

2 Letter from Louis Althusser concerning his article 'Freud and Lacan', *NLR* 55 (1969), 48.

3 Mitchell, *Women*, 52.

4 Gareth Stedman Jones, *Marxism Today*, July 1984, 39.

5 ibid., 40.

6 Chapter 1, 4.

7 We concede that Hoare's is a muddled and second-rate argument, but that does not damage our case. Had Mitchell been a man and perceived as 'non-aligned' with the *NLR* editorial board, something more distinguished would have been mounted against her (as when the board wished to rebut Eagleton's attack on Williams).

8 Hoare, 'On Women: "The Longest Revolution"', *NLR* 41 (1967) 78–81, 79.

9 We showed in the last chapter that woman tends to be produced as bourgeois whenever she appears in relation to the family. Now the same thing happens to Mitchell.

10 Hoare, ibid., 80.

11 Mitchell, *Women*, ix–x.

12 ibid., 287.

13 F. R. Leavis, *The Great Tradition* (London, 1948; Penguin edn, 1972), 39.

14 Mitchell, *Women*, 141.

15 ibid., 143.

16 Raymond Williams, *The English Novel from Dickens to Lawrence* (London: Chatto & Windus, 1970; 1974 edn), 52–4. It is interesting that this is the piece of Williams's writing to which he himself referred us as somewhere where he had tried to begin to give attention to women in his cultural theory (personal communication).

17 For a classic account of *Wuthering Heights* see A. Kettle, *An Introduction to the English Novel* (London: Hutchinson, 1951, reprinted 1969).

18 Hoare, see note 8 above.

19 Mitchell, *Women*, 289–90.

20 ibid., 292.

21 ibid., 289.

22 Catherine Clément, 'The weary sons of Freud', *Feminist Review*, 26 (1987), 51.

23 Mitchell, *Women*, 294.

24 And of course what that actually means is offering *women* for therapy, to talk *our* way out of it, to fill the gap in the male account.

25 Mitchell, *Women*, 18.

26 Letter from Louis Althusser concerning his article 'Freud and Lacan', *NLR* 55 (1969), 48.

27 Mitchell, *Women*, 249. Jane Gallop also picks up this 'reference' to Althusser as the connection between Mitchell's Marxism and her Lacanianism: 'That title has a resonant connective function since Althusser wrote a text called "Freud and Lacan". . . . With the title "Freud and Lacan: Psychoanalytic Theories of Sexual Difference", Mitchell implicitly reinscribes her introduction of Lacan in a feminist context as a repetition of Althusser's introduction of him in a Marxist context.' And again: 'Althusser is mentioned only twice in the book *Women: The Longest Revolution*: once in the preface to the 1966 essay and again, over two hundred pages later, in the preface to the introduction to *Feminine Sexuality*. Never named within an actual essay, Althusser inhabits the connective tissue, the joints which allow Mitchell to smooth over the "very different . . . very different" with "some echoes".' ('Juliet Mitchell and the "human" sciences', in T. Brennan (ed.), *Between Feminism and Psychoanalysis* (London: Routledge, 1989). But Gallop does not recognize the allusion to Williams in 'The Longest Revolution'.

28 Juliet Mitchell, *Psychoanalysis and Feminism* (Harmondsworth: Penguin, 1974), 413.

29 ibid., xv.

30 *m/f*, 8 (1982), 3–16 (interview by Parveen Adams and Elizabeth Cowie), cit. Gallop, 'Juliet Mitchell and the "human" sciences'; see Gallop for an extremely insightful set of comments on that 'return to Freud' Rose alludes to.

31 In other words, for Mitchell, originally, the female unconscious was en route to *consciousness* – consciousness was her *political* objective.

32 See e.g. Mitchell, *Psychoanalysis and Feminism*, 170–3 ('Psychoanalysis and sexuality'); J. Rose, 'Femininity and its discontents', *Feminist Review* 14 (1983) 5–21, 8.

33 Juliet Mitchell and Jacqueline Rose, *Feminine Sexuality: Jacques Lacan and the école freudienne* (London: Macmillan, 1982), 26.
34 ibid., 57.
35 *Feminist Review*, 14 (1983), 1.
36 ibid.
37 Mitchell, *Psychoanalysis and Feminism*, 410. Later (433) she specifies that Freud held the view that a woman sexually satisfied was no longer discontented.
38 J. Rose, 'Femininity and its discontents', *Feminist Review* 14 (1983) 5–21, 8.
39 Michele Barrett, *Women's Oppression Today* (London: Verso, 1980), 53.
40 ibid., 53–4.
41 Thus Barrett and Mitchell (in *Psychoanalysis and Feminism*) are in agreement with Althusser that although the 'unconscious' might usefully be considered as the place where ideology is experienced, it 'should be rechristened as soon as a better term is found'.
42 Michele Barrett, 'The concept of "difference"', *Feminist Review*, 26 (1987), 29–41, 37 and 40.
43 ibid., 40.
44 'Femininity and its discontents', 19.
45 Barrett, 'The concept of "difference"', 39.
46 R. Samuel (ed.), *People's History and Socialist Theory* (London: Routledge & Kegan Paul, 1981), 366–7.
47 ibid., 370.
48 ibid., 370–1.
49 ibid., 371.
50 E. P. Thompson, *The Poverty of Theory* (London: Merlin, 1978), 368. In the very same volume as that containing the exchange on patriarchy and women's history between Rowbotham, Alexander, and Taylor, Thompson himself reaffirmed his commitment to 'values' and 'morals' produced in terms of familial relations: 'I am . . . astonished to find that I present values and norms as "transcendental human values *outside* of real historical conditions". . . . This seems to me to indicate a serious closure or refusal which still marks the Marxist tradition. For what I actually say about this – "A materialist examination of values must situate itself, not by idealist propositions, but in the face of culture's material abode: the people's way of life, and, above all, their productive and familial relationships" (*Poverty of Theory*, p. 368) – allows no warrant for this dismissal. This continues to be . . . a central piece of my own historical *and theoretical* engagement: neither abstract, nor a-historical, nor transcendental, but contextual and materialist (E. P. Thompson, 'The politics of theory', in Samuel (ed.), *People's History and Socialist Theory*, 403).
51 See Chapter 3, pp. 60, 68.
52 See, for example, the space devoted to Thompson, one way or another, in the Raphael Samuel volume.
53 For the influence of high culture on the construction of 'values' in working-class writing see J. Swindells, *Victorian Writing and Working Women* (Cambridge: Polity Press, 1985).

54 Sally Alexander, 'Women, class and sexual differences in the 1830s and 1840s: some reflections on the writing of a feminist history', *History Workshop Journal* 17 (1983), 125–49, 131–2. For the Thompson view of consciousness she references Raphael Samuel's 'afterword' to the History Workshop volume in which Thompson is such a persistent presence.

55 ibid., 137.

56 ibid., 140.

57 ibid., 141.

58 On women's participation in Chartism see Dorothy Thompson, 'Women in nineteenth century radical politics', in J. Mitchell and A. Oakley (eds), *The Rights and Wrongs of Women* (London: Penguin, 1976), 112–38.

59 And their work is defined as inferior *because* work recognized as 'women's' is 'domestic' – the family is where they work. See next chapter.

60 Alexander, 'Women, class and sexual differences', 131.

61 See e.g. G. Stedman Jones, *Languages of Class: Studies in English Working Class History 1832–1982* (Cambridge: Cambridge University Press, 1983).

62 Alexander, 'Women, class and sexual differences', 130. Here, as in Rose, 'discontent' is shifted from its psychoanalytic sense of 'permanent state of psychic disorder' to 'voice of struggle'. It is especially clear in the break between the 'theoretical' and 'applied' parts of Alexander's article ('Perhaps this needs further elaboration. Those who prefer to move straight to the political language of working class movements in the 1830s and '40s should skip this following (selective) exegesis.') that there is some difficulty in even conceptualizing the transition from a stated intention to focus on individual subjectivity to an 'enlarged' version of political consciousness.

63 Alexander, 'Women, class and sexual differences', 127–8.

5 'Who Speaks for History?

1 Ken Worpole, 'A ghostly pavement: the political implications of local working-class history', in R. Samuel, *People's History and Socialist Theory* (London: Routledge & Kegan Paul, 1981), 22–32, 32.

2 E. P. Thompson, *The Making of the English Working Class* (London: Gollancz, 1963; Penguin edn, 1968), 12.

3 Samuel (ed.), *People's History and Socialist Theory*.

4 David Vincent, *Bread, Knowledge and Freedom: A Study of Nineteenth-Century Working Class Autobiography* (London: Methuen, 1981).

5 Popular Memory Group, 'Popular memory: theory, politics, method', in Richard Johnson, Gregor McLennan, Bill Schwarz, and David Sutton (eds), *Making Histories*, Centre for Contemporary Cultural Studies (London: Hutchinson, 1982), 231.

6 E. J. Hobsbawm, *Labouring Men: Studies in the History of Labour* (London: Weidenfeld & Nicolson, 1964; 1986 edn), vii.

7 Chapter 2, page 35.
8 See above, Chapter 3, pp. 49–50.
9 Perry Anderson, *Arguments Within English Marxism* (London: New Left Books and Verso, 1980), 158.
10 See Hobsbawm, 'The standard of living debate: a postscript', in *Labouring Men*, 120–5.
11 Hobsbawm, 'The machine breakers', in *Labouring Men*, 5–17, 5.
12 ibid., 7–10.
13 *Past and Present* 1 (1952), i.
14 Raymond Williams, *Culture and Society 1780–1950* (London: Chatto & Windus, 1958; Penguin edn, 1961), 311.
15 ibid., 312.
16 Thompson, *Making of the English Working Class*, 9.
17 ibid., 462.
18 ibid., 463.
19 ibid., 8–10.
20 ibid., 8–9.
21 ibid., 939.
22 ibid.
23 ibid., 347.
24 ibid., 351. In his 1968 'Postscript' Thompson indicates that the chapter from which we take these two formulations – 'Standards and experience' – was a direct response to the standard-of-living debate, and says that 'it now seems to me to be an ungenerous chapter' (916), but that it stands as a record of an important polemic.
25 ibid., 485.
26 ibid.
27 ibid., 486.
28 ibid., 485–6.
29 The section of *The Making of the English Working Class* in which Thompson makes this plea for 'values' in history with passion is entitled (after Blake) 'Myriads of eternity' (485–8). The culminating sentence of the entire book runs: 'Yet the working people should not be seen only as the lost myriads of eternity. They had also nourished, for fifty years, and with incomparable fortitude, the Liberty Tree. We may thank them for these years of heroic culture' (915). So the passionate plea for the retrieval of values is the crux of Thompson's argument. On moral realism, see above, Chapter 3.
30 Chapter 3, page 57.
31 Thompson, *Making of the English Working Class*, 913.
32 Chapter 3, page 57.
33 Thompson, *Making of the English Working Class*, 488.
34 Williams, *Culture and Society*, 49.
35 ibid., 56.
36 G. Stedman Jones, *Languages of Class: Studies in English Working Class History 1832–1982* (Cambridge: Cambridge University Press, 1983), 12.
37 We shall find this idea again when we come to Richard Hoggart's *The*

Uses of Literacy (London: Chatto & Windus, 1967; Penguin edn, 1958) in the next chapter.

38 Stedman Jones, *Languages of Class*, 182–3.

39 ibid., 236–7.

40 See above, Chapter 4, page 89.

41 There are similar problems with *The Maimie Papers*, ed. R. Rosen and S. Davidson (London: Virago, 1979).

42 L. Stanley (ed.), *The Diaries of Hannah Cullwick, Victorian Maidservant* (London: Virago, 1984).

43 *Diaries of Hannah Cullwick*, 1–2.

44 ibid., 4.

45 ibid., 16.

46 Cullwick refers to herself persistently in her diaries as 'drudge' to Munby's 'Massa': 'I was now a regular drudge & my hands were grimed with dirt, & big & red wi' the frost, & M[assa] told me to come to him in my dirt. . . . Massa used to pass close by on his way to Westminster daily, & he came once or twice to see me shake the mats against the lamp post in the street, & I think I look'd as poor & black a drudge as any in the street' (57). This term 'drudge' effects the elision of Cullwick's utterly subordinate working position and her total subservience within her relationship with Munby. It was a term of 'approbation' (since that is how Cullwick appears to use it) presumably selected by Munby.

47 Williams, *Culture and Society*, 316.

48 *Diaries of Hannah Cullwick*, 13.

49 ibid., 4.

50 For a fuller critique of such 'liberation', see J. Swindells, 'Liberating the subject?' A reading of the *Diaries of Hannah Cullwick*, in The Personal Narrative's Group (ed.), *Interpreting Women's Lives* (Indiana University Press, 1989).

51 *Diaries of Hannah Cullwick*, 14.

6 Culture in the Working Classroom

1 Juliet Mitchell, *Women: The Longest Revolution* (London: Virago, 1984), 128.

2 Perry Anderson, 'Components of the national culture', *New Left Review* 50 (1968), 3–57, 5.

3 E. P. Thompson, 'The politics of theory', in R. Samuel (ed.), *People's History and Socialist Theory* (London: Routledge & Kegan Paul, 1981), 396–408, 397.

4 Transcript of a recorded conversation between Richard Hoggart and Raymond Williams, from the opening issue of *New Left Review*: 'Working class attitudes', *New Left Review*, 1 (1960), 26–30, 26.

5 We are not allowed to call these Marxists 'culturalists' (though it would be convenient), because Thompson has made such a fuss about it. See R. Johnson, 'Against absolutism', in R. Samuel (ed.), *People's History and Socialist Theory* (London: Routledge & Kegan Paul, 1981), 386–96; Thompson, 'The politics of theory'.

6 Raymond Williams 'Culture and revolution: a comment', in T. Eagleton and B. Wicker (eds), *From Culture to Revolution* (London: Sheed & Ward, 1968), 22–34, 22.

7 Raymond Williams, *Politics and Letters: Interviews with New Left Review* (London: Verso, 1979), 66. In this passage (which we quoted in full in Chapter 2) Williams is extremely interesting on the undesirable seductive force of practical criticism for Left critics: 'Secondly, within literary studies themselves there was the discovery of practical criticism. That was intoxicating, something I cannot describe too strongly. Especially if you were as discontented as I then was. I said intoxication, which is a simultaneous condition of elation, excitement, and loss of measure and intelligence. Yes, it was all those things, but let me put it on record that it was incredibly exciting. I still find it exciting, and at times I have positively to restrain myself from it because actually I can do it reasonably well, I think: I've taught it to other people. Today when I am writing about a novel, it is a procedure that comes very easily to me, but I try to refrain from using it. It always tends to become too dominant a mode, precisely because it evades both structural problems and in the end all questions of belief and ideology. But at the time we thought it was possible to combine this with what we intended to be a clear Socialist cultural position. In a way the idea was ludicrous, since Leavis's cultural position was being spelt out as precisely not that. But I suppose that was why we started our own review, rather than queuing up to become contributors to *Scrutiny*.' It is difficult not to see that 'intoxication, which is a simultaneous condition of elation, excitement, and loss of measure and intelligence' as the state of feeling which succeeds the feeling of inequality, of not belonging, of being excluded (by virtue of one's class) – hence as the condition of artificially *overcoming* 'uncommunity' within English studies, of becoming acceptable. It is Williams's recognition of this, in our view, which makes him both acknowledge it and restrain himself from using it.

8 That is, we do not want to overburden this discussion with obvious parallels with Leavisism, but we do feel it necessary from time to time to point out the more startling correspondences, which have certainly made for muddle and difficulty, particularly in the education enterprise, where Leavis's goals can sound eerily like those of the Left: 'An education that conceives seriously its function in the modern world will, then, train awareness (*a*) of the general process of civilization indicated above, and (*b*) of the immediate environment, physical and intellectual – the ways in which it tends to affect taste, habit, preconception, attitude to life and quality of living. For we are committed to more consciousness; that way, if any, lies salvation. We cannot, as we might in a healthy state of culture, leave the citizen to be formed unconsciously by his environment.' (F. R. Leavis and D. Thompson, *Culture and Environment* (London: Chatto & Windus, 1933), 4–5).

9 Francis Mulhern's *The Moment of Scrutiny* (London: New Left Books, 1979) closes with a fairly passionate account of this seductive power of Leavis and *Scrutiny* for the Left: 'The most pervasive and damaging

effects of [*Scrutiny*'s cultural] power are generated at another level, in that complex of ideas that invests the apparently specialist procedures of 'literary criticism', in the discourse on 'community'. This was the source of *Scrutiny*'s profound appeal in education. . . . It has also been the source of *Scrutiny*'s quite constant appeal for the Left, over nearly fifty years. The reasons for this are not difficult to find. At the most practical and pertinent level, it was evident that *Scrutiny* had opened up an educational space within which the cultural institutions of bourgeois-democratic capitalism could be subjected to critical analysis – a space which was to be utilized to remarkable effect, most notably by Raymond Williams and the Centre for Contemporary Cultural Studies founded by Richard Hoggart at Birmingham University' (329).

10 *Scrutiny* 1 (1932), 177–8.
11 Hoggart and Williams, 'Working class attitudes', 26.
12 ibid.
13 Eagleton gives us an account of the problems in taking 'individual working-class experience' as the justification *per se* of an authentic consciousness, once the individual has moved 'out of a working-class home into an academic curriculum' (though he chooses a curious occasion on which to do so): 'In the early 1960s I went from a working-class North-of-England background to Cambridge, at a time when the university was even more male- and upper-class-dominated than it is today. . . . The group we *really* couldn't stand . . . were the English public schools socialists. . . . Who the bloody hell did they think they were, claiming our cause for themselves? They didn't have any *experience* of being working class. . . . Most of my Cambridge working-class friends are now Tories, social democrats, or political cynics. Because their politics were so closely bound to an intense bitter personal experience, they couldn't survive the changes brought about by later middle-class affluence. Most of the public-school Marxists, by contrast, are still on the Left, some of them doing substantial radical work. Their politics were also of course bound by inversion to personal experience. . . . But the connections were more complex and oblique, and in certain ways, though not in others, there had never been much in it personally for them to become socialists' ('Response [to Elaine Showalter]', in A. Jardine and P. Smith (eds), *Men in Feminism* (London: Methuen, 1987), 133–5, 133–4).
14 Hoggart and Williams, 'Working class attitudes', 26.
15 ibid., 27–8.
16 ibid., 28–9.
17 ibid., 28.
18 See our Preface.
19 Richard Hoggart, *The Uses of Literacy* (London: Chatto & Windus, 1957; Penguin edn, 1958), 37.
20 The repititious use of 'comely' is a clear case of romanticizing northern industrial life: 'comely', as in 'a comely lass'.
21 Bea Campbell, *Wigan Pier Revisited: Poverty and Politics in the 80s* (London: Virago, 1984), 222.

22 ibid., 224. See also Juliet Mitchell, *Woman's Estate* (Harmondsworth: Penguin, 1971, reprinted 1973) on families and individuals.

23 In other words, he relapses into moral realism; see our Chapter 3.

24 Hoggart, *Uses of Literacy*, 258.

25 See Williams, in *Politics and Letters* (London: New Left Books and Verso, 1981), 66, on Leavis's 'cultural radicalism'.

26 In this debate, Williams's early work played a prominent part.

27 Brian Jackson and Dennis Marsden, *Education and the Working Class: Some General Themes Raised by a Study of 88 Working-Class Children in a Northern Industrial City* (London: Routledge & Kegan Paul, 1962; revised edn, Penguin, 1966). It is worth recalling that Williams's 'long revolution' was the subject of heated exchange between Williams and Thompson, precisely because the latter rejected the idea that there could be gradual alterations to consciousness – a bloodless revolution over time.

28 This is particularly clear in the case of Jackson and Marsden: their '88 working-class children in a northern industrial city' are made up to the round figure of ninety by the addition of Jackson and Marsden themselves. 'We gathered a sample of ninety working-class children. Two of the names on that sample are Brian Jackson and Dennis Marsden. In this report we track the fortunes of the other eighty-eight – the ones we saw. But the reader, standing further back than we ever can, perceives the full ninety.'

29 Jackson and Marsden, *Education and the Working Class*, 243. The passage from Arnold claims that culture 'does away with classes': '[Culture] seeks to do away with classes; to make the best that has been thought and known in the world current everywhere; to make all men live in an atmosphere of sweetness and light, where they may use ideas, as it uses them itself, freely – nourished, and not bound by them.' The quotations within the body of the Jackson and Marsden passage are also from Arnold.

30 'The educational system we need is one which accepts and develops the best qualities in working-class living, and brings those to meet our central culture' (246).

31 Jackson and Marsden, *Education and the Working Class*, 97.

32 There seems little difference between this version of the organic and authentic values and Leavis's formulation: 'The organic community has virtually disappeared, and with it the only basis for a genuine national culture; so nearly disappeared that when one speaks of the old popular culture that existed in innumerable local variations people cannot grasp what one means. . . . The memory of the old order, the old ways of life, must be the chief hint for, the directing incitement towards, a new, if ever there is to be a new' (*Scrutiny* 1 (1932), 177–8).

33 Jackson and Marsden, *Education and the Working Class*, 59. But when it comes to categorizing their eighty-eight working-class children according to their families, particularly according to paternal occupation, they register a problem: 'We . . . examined the pass-lists of the Higher School Certificate and G.C.E. 'A' level at all the Huddersfield grammar

schools. We selected the pass-lists for the years 1949 to 1952, since the men and women on them would now be between twenty-five and thirty. This was important, because we wanted to talk to adults, many of whom would now be married and parents themselves. We expected that they would have moved along in their chosen professions, and taken their general bearings in life: the turbulence of adolescence and the possible vagaries of college days would be behind them. From these former pass-lists we then drew the names of all children whose fathers were working-class. To define this we used the Registrar-General's classification of occupations. The sample drawn like this provided us with 49 boys, but only half that number of girls. This was our first problem, and a discovery of interest.' They are being systematic about their sampling, with due attention to equal numbers of boys and girls. The fact that in the sample period twice as many working-class boys as girls feature on the pass-lists is duly registered as a sampling problem and 'a discovery of interest'. They solve the sampling problem by broadening the period for girls – 'we increased our number of girls by extending the years for them only, back to 1946 and forward to 1954'. The 'interest' of the discovery, however, surfaces for that brief moment, and then disappears again from view.

34 Williams, 'Culture and revolution: a comment', in T. Eagleton and B. Wicker (eds), *From Culture to Revolution* (London: Sheed & Ward, 1968), 22.

35 James Donald and Jim Grealy, 'The unpleasant fact of inequality: standards, literacy and culture', in Ann Marie Wolpe and James Donald (eds), *Is There Anyone Here From Education?* (London: Pluto Press, 1983), 89–90.

36 Raymond Williams, *The Long Revolution* (London: Chatto & Windus, 1961; Penguin edn, 1965), 176.

37 *New Left Review* 1 (1960), 27.

38 It is striking that the clearest, most precise critiques of this kind of version of the relationship between experience of culture come within critiques of Leavisism and the use of English literature as a source of equality in education. See for instance the following: 'The whole of [Denys Thompson's] argument depends on the acceptance of education, and English [literature] within it, as essentially aiming at the inculcation of the moral qualities of a civilized adult. . . . Firstly, he spoke of expressing "*experience*". Now experience can be an awkward subject. It is from one viewpoint wholly private and *personal*, concerned with self-expression for one's own private purposes. . . . It is from another viewpoint *cultural* in that we "experience" what we do, as a result of our upbringing in a particular time and place through a particular mediating form of language and perception. . . . Though he is not sufficiently explicit, [Denys] Thompson clearly presumes some interaction between the personal and the "cultural" experience through the medium of literature, whose subject is "focused" experience, allowing us to reflect on our own' (David Allen, *English Teaching Since 1965* (London: Heinemann, 1980, 9–10.)

39 *Screen Education* 40, Autumn/Winter (1981/2), 82.

Notes

Postscript

1 Stuart Hall, 'Only connect: the life of Raymond Williams', *New Statesman*, 5 May 1988, 20–1, 20.
2 Terry Eagleton, 'Resources for a journey of hope: the significance of Raymond Williams', *New Left Review* 168 (1988), 3–11, 3–4.
3 Stephen Heath, 'Modern English man', *The Times Higher Education Supplement*, 20 July 1984, 17.
4 Francis Mulhern, 'Living "the work"', *Guardian*, 29 January 1988.
5 'Working class attitudes', *New Left Review* 1 (1960), 26–30, 26.
6 Raymond Williams, 'Culture and a comment', in T. Eagleton and B. Wicker (eds), *From Culture to Revolution* (London: Sheed & Ward, 1968), 22–34, 22.
7 See, especially, Eagleton's response to Showalter in A. Jardine and P. Smith (eds), *Men in Feminism* (London: Methuen, 1987).
8 D. Robbins, 'A wider context for Raymond Williams', *The Times Higher Education Supplement*, 27 July 1984.
9 'Last dispatches from the border country', *Nation*, 5 March 1988.

Index